Markets of Provence

◆ **Best Markets**

ns

entoux ▲

◆ **Bédoin**

◆ **Sault**

◆ **Saint-Saturnin-lès-Apt**

◆ **Forcalquier**

◆ **Gordes**

◆ **Roussillon**

ustellet

◆ **Apt**

*Parc Naturel Régional
du Luberon*

(D900)

Manosque

◆ **Bonnieux**

◆ **Cucuron**

**Saint-Martin-
de-la-Brasque**

◆ **Lourmarin**

ce River

◆ **Cadenet**

◆ **La Tour-d'Aigues**

Pertuis

(A51)

(A8)

↓ *to Marseille*

Aix-en-Provence

© 2015 Jeffrey L. Ward

·MARKETS OF·

Provence

MARKETS OF

Provence

Food, Antiques, Crafts, and More

Text and photographs by
Marjorie R. Williams
with Dixon Long

ST. MARTIN'S GRIFFIN ❧ NEW YORK

MARKETS OF PROVENCE. Text and photographs copyright © 2016 by Marjorie R. Williams. All rights reserved. Printed in China. For information, address St. Martin's Press, 175 Fifth Avenue, New York, N.Y. 10010.

www.stmartins.com

Design by Ralph Fowler / rlfdesign

Production Manager: Adriana Coada

The Library of Congress Cataloging-in-Publication Data is available upon request.

ISBN 978-1-250-05127-1 (trade paperback)
ISBN 978-1-250-09163-5 (e-book)

Our books may be purchased in bulk for promotional, educational, or business use. Please contact your local bookseller or the Macmillan Corporate and Premium Sales Department at 1-800-221-7945, extension 5442, or by e-mail at MacmillanSpecialMarkets@macmillan.com.

First Edition: May 2016

10   9   8   7   6   5   4   3   2   1

To Michael

Le Paradis n'est pas artificiel.
—Ezra Pound

Contents

Monday Markets

Tuesday Markets

Wednesday Markets

Thursday Markets

Friday Markets

Saturday Markets

More Options

Resources

Introduction

Provence is a place of extraordinary beauty and bounty. Breath-taking landscapes, blue sky, dazzling light, and a Mediterranean climate form a magical backdrop. The region has been described in countless paintings, films, and books. And yet, much mystery remains. What's the best way to see, taste, and smell Provence?

The answer, I believe, is to visit its markets. They have been the heart of Provençal life since the Middle Ages. I began my research in 2012, returning in different seasons over a few years to see how the offerings change from summer to fall and winter to spring. I noticed similar items—and often the same vendors—appearing in multiple markets. And yet, every market is unique. Each one takes on the shape and personality of the village. Further differences emerge in local specialties, traditions, and landscapes. You don't have to be fluent in French to enjoy them. Nor must you have a kitchen or be a hard-core shopper. Instead, think of markets as a way to experience Provence—its crops, customs, crafts, and culture.

Nearly every village and town has its own market, usually open one day a week. There are nearly 200, which I've narrowed to 30 that stand out for their quality, range of goods, or something special about the setting. My focus is mainly between Aix en Provence to the south, Mont Ventoux to the north, the Alpes-de-Haute-

Provence to the east, and the Rhône River to the west. That's where there's the greatest concentration of exceptional markets.

The book is organized by day of the week so that you can easily identify which options are available on any given day. Each chapter opens with a map showing the recommended markets that day. Orange diamonds identify those that I consider the best. Purple dots indicate others that might be worth a stop if you are nearby. Some towns have more than one type of market on different days. A few, such as Les Halles d'Avignon and the market in Aix-en-Provence, are open several days weekly. In those cases, the market is described fully only once with page references to it elsewhere.

My aim is to inspire and inform you. Whether you explore one market or several, and whether on your own or as part of a group, this book will make the planning more reliable and the rewards richer. It will spare you the disappointment of being in the right place at the wrong time. Saint-Rémy is terrific anytime, but if you're there on market day (Wednesday) you'll double the fun.

The ancient Romans built bridges and roads to connect the villages. But everyone who goes to Provence cuts a unique path through this enchanted land. While it's impossible to grasp its depths in a single visit—or in a lifetime—seeing Provence through its markets reveals something essential about its soil and its soul. Come along and enjoy the journey. It will be one you'll never forget.

Types of Markets in Provence

TRADITIONAL PROVENÇAL MARKETS
(Marchés Provençaux, Marchés Hebdomadaires)

These are the most common type of market in Provence. They're held outdoors year-round (though smaller in winter), from about 8:30 a.m. to noon, usually only once a week. Vendors sell fresh ingredients, prepared foods, flowers, and souvenirs. Farmers might bring local produce; however, these are not farmers' markets in the pure sense (for that, see below). Some (*grands marchés*) are large and diverse. Others are *très petit* but still cover the basics. Village markets have a markedly different ambience from city markets.

FLEA AND ANTIQUES MARKETS
(Marchés des Antiquités, Brocantes, Puces, and Vide Greniers)

Professional dealers sell at *les marchés des antiquités*. *Brocantes* are simpler marketplaces of dealers who rove from town to town selling secondhand items. At *vide greniers* ("attic-emptiers," akin to yard sales or car-trunk sales), individuals cast off unwanted household items—often junk, but the occasional dusty treasure

COVERED MARKETS
(Les Halles)
Indoor markets are open most weekdays, both morning and afternoon. The covered structures help maintain a constant temperature. The main covered markets are in Avignon and Nîmes.

FARMERS' MARKETS
(Marchés Paysans, Marchés des Producteurs, Marchés Agricoles)
Farmers bring seasonal produce (and cheese, jams, honey, and wine) to sell directly. These markets are well supported by the locals, who appreciate the direct connection with producers. Certified organic is indicated by "AB" signage (*Agriculture Biologique*).

EVENING MARKETS
(Marchés du Soir)
Evening markets usually feature the local farmers and sometimes include an *animation* such as a cooking demonstration.

CRAFT MARKETS
(Marchés des Artisans, Marchés des Créateurs)
Local artisans sell jewelry, accessories, and other crafts. Some towns attempt to maintain a quality standard. Others have looser rules, and the tacky quotient can soar.

SPECIALTY MARKETS
Truffle markets, Christmas markets, and *santon* markets feature seasonal highlights and attract eager shoppers during the winter.

FARM VISIT MARKETS
(Marchés à la Ferme)

Many farmers participate in the *Bienvenue à la Ferme* program during the growing season, welcoming visitors to their farms.

Insider Tips

Timing. Traditional markets are busiest from 9 to 11 a.m. Most begin to close at noon. Arrive by 8:30 for the best selection and decent parking, leaving sightseeing for the afternoon. Consider whether you'll need to cross the Luberon mountain. Driving through narrow passes makes for stunning views but takes longer.

Parking. It can be a challenge. Street parking is usually free, although a few towns charge (a *hordateur* prints timed passes for a couple of euros). Blue "P" signs indicate parking lots. Always lock your vehicle and tuck valuables out of sight.

Navigating. Buy a foldout map (such as Michelin map #527) before departure to supplement any GPS device. Tourist offices provide maps of the immediate vicinity and usually sell maps of the broader region.

Language. Say *bonjour* (hello), *merci* (thank you), and *au revoir* (good-bye), even if you can't speak other French. Your effort will be appreciated. The French are more attuned to these courtesies than many other cultures.

Food markets. Look for stalls with a limited selection. Vendors with only a few items are usually local producers, while those who display a broad variety are resellers. Also notice which stands have a line of customers. A queue means that the locals prefer that vendor, and it's probably worth the wait. If you specify when you intend to eat foods that ripen, such as cheese or melons, the vendor will select items that'll be perfectly ready.

Bring. Most vendors don't accept credit cards, so bring small denominations of cash. Also bring a basket or buy one while you're at a market if you'll be going to several.

Bathrooms. There aren't any at the markets. You can go to a café and use their WC, but it's expected that you'll purchase something, which may be as simple as an espresso.

Learn as you go. Don't worry about making mistakes. The Provençal people tend to be very friendly, warm, and relaxed.

TRIBUNAL
DE
COMMERCE

Sunday

MARKETS

Best

Coustellet *(farmers' market)*

L'Isle-sur-la-Sorgue *(flea/antiques &
traditional Provençal market)*

Saint-Martin-de-la-Brasque *(farmers' market)*

Avignon *(covered market)*, see p. 161

Others

Aix-en-Provence *(monthly book market)*

Ansouis *(traditional Provençal market)*

Carpentras *(flea/antiques market)*

Châteaurenard *(traditional Provençal market)*

Nîmes *(covered market)*, see p. 213

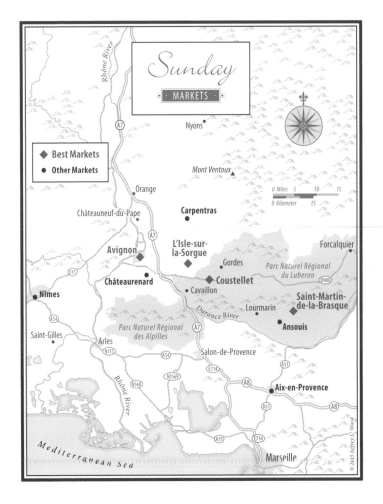

Sunday

MARKETS

Rhône River

A7

Nyons

Mont Ventoux ▲

0 Miles 5 10 15
0 Kilometer 15

◆ Best Markets
● Other Markets

Orange

Carpentras

Châteauneuf-du-Pape

A7

L'Isle-sur-la-Sorgue

Forcalquier

Avignon

Gordes

Parc Naturel Régional du Luberon

D900

Châteaurenard

Coustellet

Nîmes

Cavaillon

Saint-Martin-de-la-Brasque

E15

Durance River

Lourmarin

Ansouis

Parc Naturel Régional des Alpilles

A7

Saint-Gilles

Arles

N113

Salon-de-Provence

A51

A54

N568

N1569

A54

E714

A8

Aix-en-Provence

A51

A8

Rhône River

A55

E714

Mediterranean Sea

Marseille

© 2015 Jeffrey L. Ward

Coustellet

❖ FARMERS' MARKET ❖

WHEN: *Sunday morning from April until December*

WHERE: *Route D900 in Coustellet*

*L*OCAL RESIDENTS don't shy away from spirited debate, but one opinion that seems widely shared is that Coustellet's market is among the area's best. Sunday is the big day for this *marché paysan* (farmers' market).

Coustellet, Maubec, and Robion adjoin near the D900, creating a busy intersection by Provençal standards. The location lacks charm, but the bustling market more than makes up for its rather drab surroundings. Villagers flock here not only to shop but also to see friends and neighbors. Gossip gets traded as swiftly as the fishmonger's fresh catch passes into customers' hands. Near the market's entrance, cheerful pansies (called *pensées,* or "thoughts") greet customers like a throng of smiling faces.

The quality of this market is a big draw. If you're not sure where to go, follow people who look like they know where they are going. The largest section is dedicated to stalls run by farmers, many of whom have been coming to this market for decades. Their hands are calloused from working the land, and their faces are weathered by the elements.

Local cherries, goat cheeses, *Muscat* grapes, salad greens, olive oils, honeys, and fruit jams are just the beginning. One farmer displays eight varieties of potatoes which he sells by the kilo, but it's fine to buy them in smaller amounts. Bulbs of fresh garlic are piled into mountains; pumpkins and squashes could crush toes if they were to roll off the tables. Drinking glasses arranged in neat rows await a sample pour of local wine. Several women sell lavender sprigs tied together with purple satin ribbons known as *quenouilles tressées.*

Rolland Tranchimand's miniature vegetables attract a bevy of discerning shoppers. He picked the zucchini blossoms early this morning. Wrapping half a dozen like a delicate bouquet, he hands them to a customer who will stuff them with soft goat cheese and fry them lightly for an hors d'oeuvre. François Gregoire sells organic goat cheeses that he makes at his farm in Goult. Catherine Pisani grows more than 30 types of basil at La Ferme aux Basilics in Roussillon. When she runs out of the fresh harvest, she has other items that she makes with distilled essence of basil (see p. 176).

Along the outer aisles, stands overflow with olive-wood kitchen utensils, clothing, jewelry, hats, baskets, fabrics, and sandals. Mouthwatering rotisserie chicken, golden paella, and a pizza truck offer quick ways of satisfying appetites that have been stoked by tantalizing aromas. At Poissonerie du Luberon, the seller wears a straw hat and nautical blue-and-white-striped jersey; he'll shuck oysters if you ask.

The old *gare,* still identified by the Maubec train station sign, is now a café. A musician strums his guitar and sings "Hallelujah." Everyone rejoices at the opportunity to spend a Sunday morning at the Coustellet market.

Lavender

Provence conjures up images of lavender etching purple lines across the French countryside. If you're lucky enough to visit in summer, you can see fields carpeted with blooms.

The lavender-like plant grown at lower elevations is *lavandin,* a sterile hybrid form with a slight camphor-like scent. Pure lavender, or *lavande fin,* grows only at higher altitudes (600–2000 meters), such as around Sault. Since insects have become a big problem, growers are planting at higher elevations to avoid the pests. They're forbidden to use chemical pesticides in consideration of the bees. Fine lavender is becoming rare, and more fields are getting planted with the hardier *lavandin*. A way to tell the two apart is that each stem of *lavande fin* has a single flower, while *lavandin* has three flowers.

Lavender's growing season conveniently coincides with the peak of tourism. The Luberon valley begins lighting up with blue blooms in late June and continues until early August. The cycle runs about two weeks later in higher elevations, from July until mid-August. The lavender fields at Abbaye de Sénanque, near Gordes, are technically *lavandin*, but that doesn't make the sight any less spectacular to behold. Peak times are late June through July. I also recommend a visit to Sault (which holds a lavender festival on August 15) or follow the Lavender Route, a circuit that passes fields and distilleries. A lavender museum in Coustellet explains how the plants are cultivated and the distillation process.

L'Isle-sur-la-Sorgue

· FLEA AND ANTIQUES MARKET ·

· TRADITIONAL PROVENÇAL MARKET ·

WHEN: *Sunday (Flea and Antiques Market open most of the day; Traditional Provençal Market open in the morning only)*

WHERE: *Flea and antiques vendors on Avenue des Quatre Otages. Antiques shops on Avenue des Quatre Otages and Avenue de la Libération. Food vendors in Place de la Liberté and throughout the old town.*

OFFICE DE TOURISME: *Place de la Liberté, 84800 L'Isle-sur-la-Sorgue. A local map and Guide des Antiquaires are indispensable if you're going to explore the antiques shops. Tel: 04.90.38.04.78. www.oti-delasorgue.fr*

ENTERING L'ISLE-SUR-LA-SORGUE, one of the prettiest towns in Provence, you may think you've stepped into the pages of a well-illustrated storybook. Canals encircle the old town like an emerald necklace. Moss-covered waterwheels dip wooden paddles into the fast-flowing streams. Ducks glide along, pausing to flutter their wings or warm themselves in the sun. The scenery is so magical that it wouldn't come as a shock to see an elf or fairy peek out from a curtain of leaves.

As its name suggests, L'Isle-sur-la-Sorgue is an island on the

Sorgue River. When the popes were based in Avignon during the 15th century, local fishermen were spared taxes in exchange for donating the best of their catch to the clergy. Years later, factories harnessed the river's power to grind grain or produce wool, paper, and silk products. Only one factory still operates: Brun de Vian-Tiran has been making luxurious wool items since 1808.

For a large and friendly market with a variety of attractions, L'Isle-sur-la-Sorgue is hard to beat. If you're interested in antiques, Sunday is the day to go. There's also an open-air food market on Thursday, but with none of the antiques.

Navigating this market can be confusing for first-timers. Here's a rough overview: The island is the heart of the old city, and that's where you'll find a concentration of food and souvenir stalls. At the edge of the island, itinerant dealers display their antiques. Along Avenue des Quatre Otages and Avenue de la Libération, antiques shops and galleries cluster in "villages." Let's take a closer look.

ANTIQUES AND FLEA MARKET

L'Isle-sur-la-Sorgue is the biggest and best known of Provence's antiques markets. It's the second largest in France, after Le Marché aux Puces de Saint-Ouen in Paris (also known as Clignancourt), and third largest in Europe, after London. L'Isle-sur-la-Sorgue's reputation as an antiques center grew in 1966 after several dealers got together to host a fair. It was a success and eventually developed into a weekly affair, drawing more shopkeepers and roving vendors.

Flea and antiques vendors line the sidewalk along Avenue des

Quatre Otages. Within the span of a single block, you might find an antique baby crib, handblown wine jugs, brass bed frames, vintage linens, and an oxen yoke. Should you set your heart on larger items, shipping can be arranged.

If you haven't found any treasures with your name on them at the roving vendors' stalls, don't despair. Plenty more antiques—350 dealers and decorators, in fact—await in the shops and galleries in the direction of the train station. Ten antiques villages, or enclaves of dealers, are like small neighborhoods with restaurants and oddball flourishes. Look for signs indicating *antiquaires,* although the entrances aren't always well marked. Don't hesitate to amble into gravel courtyards. They often lead to more dealers.

Le Village des Antiquaires de la Gare, established in 1973, was the first antiques village in L'Isle-sur-la-Sorgue. It contains about 80 shops. Styles range from classical to French country to modern. In the antiques village Le Quai de la Gare, Nicole Philibert specializes in fine antiques and paintings from the 18th and 19th centuries. La Maison de Viktor offers a contrasting style with items forged out of metal, such as a *portemanteau* with *pétanque* balls as a decorative element. Interspersed among the antiques shops are art galleries. Galerie Léoni, in Carré des Arts du Luberon, is owned by the grandson of the painter Auguste Chabaud.

The antiques shops and galleries offer a vast range of paintings, tapestries, furniture, old photographs, floor tiles, garden planters, and statuary. They are typically open Saturday, Sunday, and Monday but closed other days so that dealers can scour the countryside for inventory or fix up items for sale.

It's rare to find real bargains in L'Isle-sur-la-Sorgue. Many items, however, are one-of-a-kind and quintessentially Provençal. Even though prices are on the high side, if you enjoy antiques you won't want to miss this Sunday market.

L'Isle-sur-la-Sorgue also hosts major antiques fairs every Easter weekend and the August 15 holiday, when the number of international dealers and shoppers quadruples.

TRADITIONAL PROVENÇAL MARKET

If food stalls interest you, explore that part of the market first. Food vendors start closing around noon while antiques dealers stay open through the afternoon. Cross any footbridge over the canal and make your way toward the innermost part of the old town, Place de la Liberté.

The most established stands at Provençal markets are often near churches; the prized location goes to sellers who have been coming for years. That rule of thumb applies here, with vendors surrounding the old church Nôtre-Dame-des-Anges. (Peek inside for a look at its Baroque architecture and ornate decorations.) The Office de Tourisme, next to the church in a former granary, can provide shop listings and other useful information. It closes at 1 p.m.

An olive vendor garnishes bowls to call attention to the accent flavor in the marinade. A border of red peppers, for example, signals olives with a punch of *piment d'Espelette*. *Saucissons* emit a whiff of fennel. Banon cheeses, wrapped in chestnut leaves, give off an earthy aroma. A bread vendor sells golden *fougasses* dotted

with olives, onions, and anchovies. A man slices thick slabs of fruit jellies; the fig version pairs nicely with cheese. At Pluie de Senteurs, baskets brim with herbs, spices, and seasoning salts.

More vendors sell everything from straw hats to soaps to nougat. A man pedals a machine that sharpens knives, a process known as *affûtage*. He leans forward to position a blade on the strap. Once he's done, he slices pieces of newspaper or shaves a few hairs off his forearm to demonstrate how sharp it is.

OTHER HIGHLIGHTS

To top off the outing to L'Isle-sur-la-Sorgue's market, it's worth checking out the notable shops or staying for a meal. (Restaurant suggestions are provided at the end of this book.) Leyris, an *artisan boulanger* on Rue Carnot, makes the kind of breads you might have dreamed of when you booked a trip to Provence. A few paces away at 2 Rue Louis Lopez is the exceptional chocolate shop La Cour aux Saveurs, owned by Florian Courreau, an artisan *chocolatier.* He creates a new flavor each month. Among the temptations are chocolates sprinkled with Camargue sea salt and Roches du Luberon nougat candies, colored like the red rocks around Roussillon and flavored with lavender and honey. At Lilamand, also on Rue Carnot, a specialty is *fruits confits.* Un Jour at 8 Place Ferdinand Buisson sells luxury items, including woolen items made by the local mill Brun de Vian-Tiran.

One of my favorite shops is La Manufacture, where 30 artists sell everything from raku pottery to whimsical decorations, lighting, furniture, and clothing. Outside the shop (on the walkway

Hôtel de Palerme, off Rue de la République), there's usually an exhibit designed by one of the artists, such as tail-wagging dogs fashioned out of rubber boots. Florel en Provence, at 25 Avenue de la Libération, sells organic teas in pretty tins, as well as local sea salts, honeys, and perfumes that will evoke the scent of Provence long after you've departed.

A classic spot for soaking up the market ambience is Café de France in Place de la Liberté. Some restaurants and cafés offer a view of the canals, where waterwheels make a mesmerizing backdrop. Wine bars, such as Caveau de la Tour de L'Isle and Place aux Vins, offer a good selection in a relaxed setting where customers can nibble on cheese or charcuterie.

The first Sunday of August is celebrated with a special Floating Market. Flat-bottomed boats parade on the river and angle over to the docks to sell food and flowers. It's a festive scene with traditional costumes and music. If you hear strands of "La Coupo Santo," you might be tempted to join the chorus which praises Provence.

There are numerous excursions within easy range of L'Isle-sur-la-Sorgue. Biking and hiking trails lead to villages along the Sorgue's watery path, referred to collectively as the Pays des Sorgues. The Sorgue River begins at Fontaine de Vaucluse. The Fondation Poppy et Pierre Salinger in Le Thor has exhibitions, a sculpture garden, and a restaurant. The Musée de la Lavande is only a few kilometers away from L'Isle-sur-la-Sorgue in Coustellet. The tour takes about 45 minutes, or skip the explanations and go directly to the boutique, where the walls are painted shades of lavender and every imaginable lavender product is for sale.

Shopping for Antiques

The term "French country," when scrawled on sales tags far outside of France, evokes dreamy associations even when it's stretching the truth. But in Provence, it's usually a fair description of the provenance of household and farming items that are passed down through generations. They might not be fancy, but there's beauty in their simple lines and sturdy craftsmanship. Rustic furnishings, linens, and tools make Provence a haven for antiques shoppers.

Where to Find Them

❦ Antiques and flea markets in L'Isle-sur-la-Sorgue (p. 19), Villeneuve-lèz-Avignon (p. 250), Arles (p. 136), Carpentras (p. 37), and others described in this book.

❦ Antiques shops. L'Isle-sur-la-Sorgue has a dense concentration, but they're common along roadways. One of my favorites is Galerie de la Gare in Mollégès on Route D99 near Saint-Rémy, and several along the road connecting L'Isle to Le Thor.

❦ Major antiques fairs during Easter weekend and on August 15, especially in L'Isle-sur-la-Sorgue.

Even the smallest villages host occasional *brocantes* and *vide-greniers*. Watch for roadside posters announcing them or inquire at Offices de Tourisme.

Other Tips

 Know what you're getting. Antique linens are folded to present the best side. A coat of dark brown shoe polish can make a drawer look like old wood when, in fact, it was cut and fitted only a few days ago. Inspect items carefully.

 Bargaining. It's fine to negotiate, but always do so courteously. If you start too low or demand a specific price, the dealer would rather turn you away than make a sale. I generally begin at 25–30 percent below asking and settle for 10–20 percent, if I can get it.

 Shipping. Established dealers work with shippers and can assist with arrangements. Know the options and prices before you seal the deal. Ask if large purchases can be exempt from VAT. Paperwork is involved, but the savings can be significant.

Shadowing Chef Cédric Brun
at Les Halles d'Avignon

A theme that repeatedly comes up in conversations with Provençal chefs is how much they enjoy working with local ingredients. Cédric Brun, chef and owner of Le Carré d'Herbes in L'Isle-sur-la-Sorgue, shops at the covered market Les Halles d'Avignon to select some items directly, supplementing the deliveries he receives. I ask if I can tag along. He consents, and I jump at the chance to shadow a professional chef.

I wasn't doing much jumping, however, when the alarm went off at 5 a.m. so I could meet him by 6, the time he normally begins. (He is long gone before the market opens to the general trade at 8.) It is pitch black outside, and I wonder if I'm still dreaming as men parade with sides of beef they're unloading from trucks. My senses jolt awake as soon as I step inside the market, abuzz with conversation and the rapid movement of shopkeepers stocking their stalls.

Chef Brun knows exactly which ones he'll visit and has a good idea of what he will buy, although he remains open to influence. "It's exciting to discover what looks particularly fresh and to hear the vendors' recommendations," he says. Those relationships are the reason he continues shopping at this market despite his demanding schedule.

Our first stop is Le Boeuf Qui Rit. The lamb comes from Aveyron, beef from Nantes, and veal from Limoges. Everything, in other words, is French bred and raised, a quality that the chef values. Next we head to Maison Feste for *charcuterie*. Paper-thin slices of *jambon Ibérico* have a nutty flavor and practically melt in the mouth. The chef

chooses ivory-hued strips of pork that he'll lay atop *oeuf cocotte*.

At La Maison du Fromage, we taste a cheddar fortified with Guinness beer. Chef Brun's personal favorites are the creamy Mont d'Or and the Délice du Ministre, a goat cheese. Red and silvery fish make a shimmery display at La Marée Provençale, our next stop. The catch comes from Sète, along the Mediterranean, or from the Brittany coast. Chef Brun buys *cabillaud* (codfish). At Serge Olives, he selects olives, cured peppers, and tapenades, which will add zing to appetizers and main courses.

The chef knows the shopkeepers, and they know his tastes. They greet each other with warmth, respect, and good-humored banter. These friendships have developed from years of repeating this ritual.

He completes his shopping in 20 minutes but permits himself one final stop at Cantine Buvette. Chef Brun orders an iced tea—an unusual request for a Frenchman, especially in winter. He explains that he rarely has time to make himself a hot beverage, so he has grown accustomed to cold ones. He gulps it down, then hurries off, expertly weaving a path through the labyrinthine market.

Le Carré d'Herbes is at 13 Avenue des 4 Otages, 84800 L'Isle-sur-la-Sorgue. Tel: 04.90.38.23.97. www.lecarre dherbes.edu

Saint-Martin-de-la-Brasque

WHEN: *Sunday morning from May to October*

WHERE: *Near the town hall*

Much as Coustellet is the farmers' market of choice on Sunday morning in the northern Luberon, the Saint-Martin-de-la-Brasque market enjoys a similar reputation in the southern Luberon. It is smaller than Coustellet's market but in certain respects surpasses it in quaint charm. Fewer tourists have discovered the market in Saint-Martin-de-la-Brasque, perhaps because they've been diverted to the Sunday market in L'Isle-sur-la-Sorgue. But those who do venture here might feel as if they've stumbled upon a gem.

Sellers and shoppers take equal pleasure in coming here on Sunday morning. Locals from the village and nearby hamlets greet each other with backslaps or handshakes, and sometimes *la bise*—the Provençal variety is three lightning-quick touches of the cheek (left-right-left). Amid all the conviviality, the line occasionally blurs between who is buying and who is selling.

Unlike some markets in Provence, this one is straightforward to navigate. Vendors set up in a parking area. Wide aisles and the generous shade of plane trees contribute to the comfort. Children

squeal as they pedal bicycles, while others are drawn to a playing field next to the market. A group of young mothers huddles, delighted by the chance to socialize.

Some vendors decorate their tables with cloths that look like they've been dipped in the landscape: bright yellow, green, and red designs are decorated with the unofficial symbol of Provence, a *cigale*. But there's nothing fussy or fancy about this market. Farmers sit on empty crates during lulls between customers. Their dungarees are stained with the soil of the fields.

About 30 *producteurs* (local farmers and producers) bring fresh produce, goat cheeses, honeys, jams, meats, plants, flowers, and wines. The fruits and vegetables are the season's best: asparagus, potatoes, beans, eggplants, garlic, tomatoes, and herbs, depending on the season. If you're looking for a melon, tell the farmer when you plan to eat it and you'll be handed one that will be ripe when you're ready for it.

A woman selling vegetable and meat pies learned the recipes from her grandmother. I opt for the Basquaise with chicken, onions, tomatoes, peppers, and chorizo. Thierry and Sophie Perez raise goats in Peypin d'Aigues and sell cheeses. They handle the whole production process from "*ah*" to "*zed,*" Thierry explains. I buy a creamy round, and then honey from another *producteur* to drizzle on it later.

Sunday is family day, and a family outing to the market is often a prelude to a large meal. Two girls parade around holding up lollipops as they march to the beat of an imaginary band. A man leads his grandsons to the *coquillages* truck where he explains the differences in size, shape, and flavor of oysters from Sète. A couple sits at a table piled with empty oyster shells next to a nearly empty bottle of wine. It might be Sunday morning, but it's not too early to enjoy the local bounty. I can't resist. I purchase half a dozen oysters, squeeze a spritz of lemon on them, and savor the salty Mediterranean with every slurp.

After finishing the market, I wander into the center of the small village. Old stone buildings are brightened by red and pink geraniums on the windowsills. Lunch at Restaurant de la Fontaine makes the outing complete. Its menu features market ingredients and local wines at reasonable prices. The market baskets on the ground next to some customers are so full that they tip to one side, as if they've had a bit too much to drink.

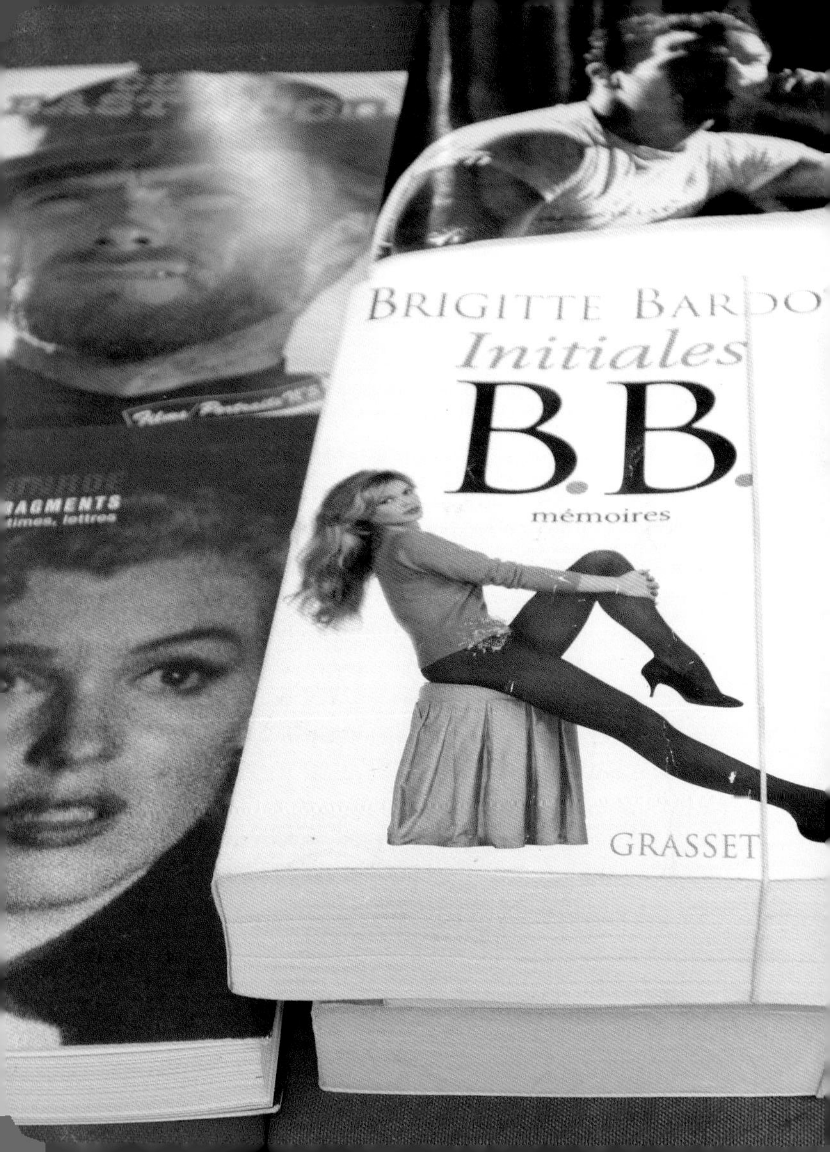
BRIGITTE BARDOT
Initiales
B.B.
mémoires
GRASSET
RAGMENTS

· OTHER SUNDAY MARKETS ·

Aix-en-Provence

❧ MONTHLY ANTIQUARIAN BOOK MARKET ❧

WHEN: *The first Sunday of every month, about 9 a.m.–4 p.m.*

WHERE: *Place de l'Hôtel de Ville*

OPEN-AIR MARKETS grace the streets and squares of Aix-en-Provence every day of the week (see p. 151), but the market for rare and secondhand books (*marché du livre ancien et d'occasion*) is monthly. If you happen to be near Aix on the first Sunday of the month, you can immerse yourself in a tradition of browsing and perhaps discover a rare edition or a topic that delights. There are books for readers of all ages and interests, from children's novels to medical tomes.

Place de l'Hôtel de Ville is filled not only with literary treasures but also with architectural marvels: elaborately carved wooden doors and lion-head knockers on the town hall, and a clock tower with a sundial and astrological clock. Sunday is a perfect day to see Aix-en-Provence at its most relaxed and enjoy the fountains, elegant squares, and winding streets.

Ansouis

WHEN: *Sunday morning*

WHERE: *Place du Lavoir*

*L*OCATED BETWEEN Lourmarin and La Tour d'Aigues, Ansouis might be worth a stop if you happen to be in the area. The village has pretty gardens and impressive views from its medieval château. Unfortunately the market isn't integrated with the most picturesque vantage points, and only a handful of vendors show up, yet they cover the basic needs: fruits and vegetables, meats, eggs, and *tartes du Luberon* stuffed with apricots. The *charcuterie* vendor sings while arranging his display. The butcher lazily sweeps leaves off the pavement and joins in the chorus, proving that the Provençal spirit bursts forth even at the smaller markets.

Carpentras

❧ · FLEA AND ANTIQUES MARKET · ❧

WHEN: *Sunday, about 10 a.m.–6 p.m.*

WHERE: *Avenue Jean Jaurès in parking lot Allée des Platanes*

*T*HIS SPRAWLING FLEA MARKET offers a chance to spend a leisurely Sunday foraging for treasures. About a hundred sellers show up in good weather. They are not professional dealers but individuals trying to unload rag-tag items. The offerings typically include kitchenware, ceramics, agricultural tools, old furniture, and linens. Perhaps you'll get lucky and spot a Provençal quilt known as a *boutis*. Sometimes children join in the fun and bring boxes of toys and clothing that they've outgrown. Items from regions far beyond Provence often show up as well.

Châteaurenard

· SMALL PROVENÇAL MARKET ·

WHEN: *Sunday morning*

WHERE: *Cours Carnot*

THIS VILLAGE NEAR AVIGNON takes its name from a *château* built in the 12th century by a feudal landowner named Reynardus. The castle overlooked the Durance River and provided protection from enemy attacks but was mostly destroyed during the French Revolution.

Châteaurenard has a small market on Sunday morning that should not be confused with its large MIN (Marché d'Intérêt National), a wholesale market. That distribution center processes about 130,000 tons of fruits and vegetables annually from area producers, going to open-air markets, restaurants, and supermarkets all over France in boxes labeled "Châteaurenard." Negotiations start at 5 a.m., and transactions proceed, category by category, for 90 minutes.

If you show up at the village market on Sunday, you'll see a tiny fraction of the melons, tomatoes, and apricots that get traded in hundreds of kilos at the MIN. Some shoppers seek out local specialties such as Frigolet, an herbal liqueur, and chocolates in the shape of small cobblestones, called *pavés du Cours Carnot*.

Breads of Provence

Fresh-baked bread is sacred to the French lifestyle. Locals usually buy one or more loaves daily. Country breads are typically made with unbleached flour and sometimes studded with olives or other additions. They're usually described by their shape and distinctive ingredients. If

you'd like your bread sliced, request "*Tranché, s'il vous plaît.*" Here are some varieties that you might find at *boulangeries* or market stands.

Shapes

Baguette	Long crusty loaf
Bâtard	Shorter and wider than a baguette, but similar consistency
Boule	Round and sometimes quite large
Ficelle	Very thin
Fougasse	Flat bread (similar to Italian *focaccia*) brushed with olive oil
Gibassier	Sturdy oval bread (originally fashioned to fit in the bags of shepherds and hunters without crumbling) made with olive oil, anise, and orange-blossom water

Ingredients

Céréale	Multigrain
Complet	Whole wheat

Épautre	Spelt
Graine	Seed
Levain	Sourdough
Noix	Nuts
Oignon	Onion
Seigle	Rye
Son	Bran

Special-Occasion Bread

Pompe à l'huile	Similar to Gibassier but softer and moister; one of the 13 desserts of the traditional Christmas meal

Monday

· MARKETS ·

Best

Bédoin *(traditional Provençal market)*

Cadenet *(traditional Provençal market)*

Fontvieille *(traditional Provençal market)*

Forcalquier *(traditional Provençal market)*

Velleron *(farmers' market)*, see p. 133

Others

Lauris *(traditional Provençal market)*

Nîmes *(flea/antiques market)*

Saint-Didier *(traditional Provençal market)*

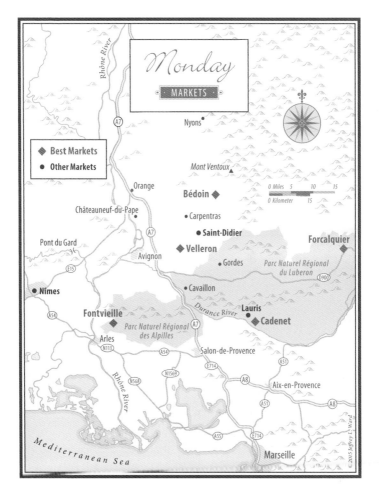

Monday
MARKETS

Best Markets ◆
Other Markets ●

Rhône River

Nyons •

Mont Ventoux ▲

Orange

Bédoin ◆

Châteauneuf-du-Pape

• Carpentras

● **Saint-Didier**

Pont du Gard

◆ **Velleron**

Avignon

• Gordes

Forcalquier ◆

Parc Naturel Régional
du Luberon

• **Nîmes**

• Cavaillon

Durance River

Fontvieille

Lauris

◆ **Cadenet**

Parc Naturel Régional
des Alpilles

Arles

Salon-de-Provence

Rhône River

Aix-en-Provence

Mediterranean Sea

Marseille

0 Miles 5 10 15
0 Kilometer 15

© 2015 Jeffrey L. Ward

Bédoin

WHEN: *Monday morning*

WHERE: *Along Avenue Barral des Baux in the village center*

OFFICE DE TOURISME: *1 Route de Malaucène, 84410 Bédoin. Tel: 04.90.65.63.95. www.bedoin.org*

BÉDOIN LIES AT THE FOOT of Mont Ventoux, nicknamed the Giant of Provence and legendary as one of the most grueling climbs in the Tour de France. The top of Mont Ventoux appears from a distance as a snowy peak but is actually a bald crown of limestone. The mountain keeps watch over this festive market like a benevolent deity. It slopes into vineyards, orchards, and dense cedar forests. The church of Saint-Antonin looms over the village with Spanish-style architecture, but the wrought-iron belfry couldn't be more typical of Provence. The closer one gets, roads become narrow and some are cordoned off on market day. If driving, park in one of the municipal lots (often large fields) a short walk away.

Bédoin is a magnet for bicyclists, who begin their steep ascent to the summit from here. Some have just returned from the invigorating downhill ride, sporting helmet-flattened hair and bringing ravenous appetites. At one entrance a vendor sells soaps in vanilla, honey, lavender, and verbena. You can mix and match your favorite combinations. Cotton clothing and Provençal fabrics practically beg to be touched. Conversations could be a soundtrack from the Tower of Babel: French, Dutch, German, Flemish, Japanese, and English (in British, Australian, American, and Canadian accents). The delights keep changing as one advances through the market: olives marinated in fennel, chewy nougat with almonds or pistachios, cheeses with soft, creamy innards that begin to ooze from the rind as the morning warms them up.

The Bédoin market is a *grand marché,* which means it offers everything one might hope for at a Provençal market. It occurs year-round, though there are more vendors from Easter to the end of September, as with other open-air markets. Gaiety fills Avenue Barral des Baux and spills into the wide plazas of Place de la Vigneronne and Place de la République. Dogs pause longingly next to *charcuterie* stands. Children dance in front of a guitarist who strums lively tunes.

Market baskets are one of my favorite souvenirs. Most are made in North Africa, but they evoke the local landscape and its bounty: deep purples of *aubergine,* oranges of *abricot,* and blues of *lavande.* Pottery also comes in Provençal colors. Many pieces have a flourish of olives, cherries, or cicadas as part of their design. Wooden toys, olive-wood utensils, *herbes de Provence,* and spiced salts make pleasing and inexpensive gifts.

Among the area's specialties are Muscat du Ventoux (dark table grapes), fruit preserves, nougat, saffron, and wines that have earned their own appellation (AOC Ventoux). At *poissonnerie* Le Relais des Mers, a fishmonger hands shucked oysters to three women.

They laugh as the briny juices drip onto their clothing. Local *producteurs* sell fresh figs, cheeses, rustic breads, olives, tapenades, and *saucissons*—ample provisions for a picnic in the countryside.

Take a short side trip to Crillon-le-Brave, a secluded village with a rocky promontory that's ideal for viewing the mountains. Its population dipped low in the 1960s, but it's experiencing a renaissance. At the top of the hill, Hôtel Crillon le Brave (a Relais & Château luxury hotel) has a casual bistro, Le Petit Crillon, which offers moderately priced lunch in a pleasant setting near a fountain.

Cadenet

WHEN: *Monday morning*

WHERE: *Village center*

OFFICE DE TOURISME: *11 Place du Tambour d'Arcole, 84160 Cadenet. Tel: 04.90.68.38.21. www.ot-cadenet.com*

CADENET WAS THE FIRST MARKET I visited in Provence. My heart quickened as I approached, driving up a slight hill from the valley and passing homes with shutters painted cheerful blues, greens, and reds. Villagers clutching straw baskets made a beeline toward the market. That was a signal to find the first available parking space. A few minutes later I was taking my first bite of *saucisson d'Arles*. As the thin slice of sausage released a rush of pepper and garlic, I was immediately and forever hooked on Provençal markets.

The town isn't especially pretty, yet it has the pleasing qualities of a typical Provençal village. It bends around cliffs, some with caves that were inhabited, and sprawls over a hilltop. There wasn't much left of the castle after it was sacked and burned during the French Revolution, but no harm came to its sweeping views of the Durance River and the Luberon countryside. In the foreground, the church tower of Saint-Étienne pierces the clear blue sky. Across the street, men play *boules* to pass the time.

Each time I return to this market, I look for *saucissons,* dry-cured sausages made of pork and other meats, then rolled in Provençal herbs or flavored with chunks of figs, mushrooms, or blue cheese. Cut open a *baguette,* smear it with butter, add slices of *saucisson* and a few gherkins, and *voilà*—you've got yourself a Provençal lunch.

In addition to *saucissons,* I am wild about market baskets. And so another reason that I feel a fondness for Cadenet is that it was a center for basketmaking. The village's name probably came from *cade,* the Provençal word for wicker. Scores of workers were based in Cadenet in the late 18th century, harvesting willow branches from the floodplains of the Durance and weaving them into baskets and furniture. The craft disappeared once foreign competition and a burgeoning plastics industry made it impossible to compete. Cadenet's last workshop closed in 1978, but a small museum (Musée de la Vannerie) in a former *atelier* displays examples of the wickerwork and provides historical background.

Cadenet's market is relatively small and caters to the local residents. The activity begins in Place du Tambour d'Arcole, with its statue of a drummer boy named André Estienne. Market stalls continue up Cours Voltaire, and more stands are in Place du 4 Septembre. Simply follow the flow of shoppers who have been carving grooves in the pavers of this route since 1566, when an edict declared Monday as Cadenet's market day. In autumn, the produce stands are filled with squashes in a variety of colors and shapes. The Muscade de Provence is a squash that's ripe even when its skin is mostly green. A vendor slices one open, revealing its orange flesh and releasing a pumpkin aroma. In spring, you'll find

AU
TAMBOUR D'ARCOLE
(ANDRÉ ESTIENNE)
ENFANT DE CADENET
1777 – 1838

SOUSCRIPTION NATIONALE

fresh strawberries and fat spears of asparagus. Cavaillon melons and plump tomatoes steal the spotlight in summer.

Chickens from a farm in nearby Mérindol turn on the rotisserie, their glistening skin a deeper golden brown with each rotation. The meat is moist and well seasoned. A pizza vendor spreads a thin layer of tomato sauce on a disc of dough, tops it with olives and anchovies, and bakes it to order in his truck. Asian *traiteurs* offer noodle dishes and egg rolls.

Nonedible items are equally diverse: clothing, belts, shoes, hats, rolls of lace, and fabric. There is nothing fancy or original, but prices are low. Most vendors are catering to the practical needs of villagers and not to tourists. They do it well, and that authenticity is another reason I enjoy this market.

The Bar du Cours in Place du 4 Septembre offers a chance for refreshment. I sip a *café noisette* (a shot of espresso with a dollop of milk, making it the color of a hazelnut) at an outdoor table. The voices of strolling shoppers blend into the gentle harmonies of a village's weekly ritual, and I feel content to be part of it this fine morning.

Cadenet also hosts a small farmers' market on Saturday morning from May until December at the *boules* court behind the church.

Fontvieille

WHEN: *Monday and Friday morning*

WHERE: *Avenue des Moulins in the village center*

OFFICE DE TOURISME: *Avenue des Moulins,*
13990 Fontvieille. Tel: 04.90.54.67.49.
www.fontvieille-provence.com

*A*N OLD DEUX CHEVAUX happens to be parked near the market's entrance when I visit one day. Made by Citroën after World War II, the car bears some resemblance to the market: it's simple, practical, and low-cost. Nothing showy, yet it has strong appeal. I was interested to learn that one of the original design specs for the car's suspension system was that it must allow a farmer to transport a basket of eggs over a plowed field without breaking any. (Another was that the interior space must be large enough to carry 50 kilograms of potatoes!)

Fontvieille is located in the heart of the Alpilles, surrounded by groves of olive trees. The village is renowned for its stone. Large slabs were used to construct the arenas at Arles and Nîmes and, more recently, the Bourse in Marseille. Homeowners throughout Provence boast of their stone coming from the Fontvieille quarries, if they can.

Another source of local pride is that novelist Alphonse Daudet

(1840–97) wrote his *Lettres de Mon Moulin* (Letters from my Windmill) here. Daudet was born in Nîmes but adopted Fontvieille as his literary home. His stories describe the everyday lives of Provençal people and are said to have been inspired by shepherds' tales. The celebrated windmill is about a 10-minute walk from the village center over some rough terrain but offers stunning views.

Twice weekly, this village revs up as shoppers and vendors go about their market rituals. Vendors set up stands along a wide aisle. Farmers bring fresh produce and eggs. Artichokes look tempting. Nougat made with local honey, almonds, and fruit is soft and chewy, but not so sticky that I risk any dental disasters. Typical market foods can be found here, including pizza, *tarte aux champignons,* and *poulet aux tomates confits.*

Shoppers saunter in and out. Locals who've finished their rounds meet with friends at Le Café. As I prepare to leave I see the Deux Chevaux still parked in the same spot, its curved hood and protruding headlights glinting brightly. It's as iconically French as the markets: a bit old-fashioned perhaps, but still relevant, functional, beloved, and timeless.

Forcalquier

WHEN: *Monday morning*

WHERE: *Town center and numerous side streets*

OFFICE DE TOURISME: *13 Place du Bourguet.*
Tel: 04.92.75.10.02. www.forcalquier.com

*P*ART OF FORCALQUIER'S ALLURE IS being off the beaten path. Located at the eastern edge of the Luberon, Forcalquier's hilly terrain is a contrast to the broad valleys of the Vaucluse. During one visit, I set out from Gordes, and the hour-long drive goes quickly. A steady ascent begins just beyond Apt. Near Céreste, an *allée* of chestnut trees bestows blessings upon all who pass beneath its leafy arms. Villages become farther separated as the road turns northward. The scenery becomes a mosaic of farms with tractors and horses, and vineyard plantings that look like they were drawn with a ruler. In summer, lavender washes the air with sweet perfume. By fall, sun-drenched leaves are turning yellow. Plumes rise as farmers burn old vine trimmings. The smoky smell foretells winter. As one approaches Forcalquier, the chapel of Notre-Dame-de-Provence comes into view, beckoning all to complete the journey to the top of the hill.

Forcalquier is possibly the biggest and best market in the Alpes-de-Haute-Provence. It started in the Middle Ages. The Counts

of Forcalquier, who permitted many freedoms, encouraged commerce along the trading routes to Spain and Italy. The town prospered as the capital of Haute Provence. Although its grandeur has faded, the town's former prestige is still visible in monuments as well as in the architectural details of some doorways and balconies.

On Monday morning a lively scene greets all comers, spilling onto sidewalks and drifting into side streets. Market stalls take over the Place du Bourguet next to the 12th-century church Notre-Dame-du-Bourguet. More are in Place Vieille, Place Martial Sicard, and Place Saint-Michel. Craftsmen and others sell accessories in the Cour des Artisans.

The area is known for attracting free spirits, who began settling here after the student uprisings in 1968. Their presence contributes to a thriving cultural and arts scene, and many come to sell homemade or homegrown products. *Païs Alp* signs indicate items from the nearby countryside, including organic vegetables, grains, and breads such as *pain à l'Ancienne*.

Local cheeses are a popular item at this market, especially the *fromage de Banon,* AOP goat's milk cheese from nearby Banon. One vendor sells cheeses that he dipped in wine before wrapping them in chestnut leaves. Signs indicate how long the cheeses have been aging—10, 12, or 15 days—strengthening their flavor.

Honey is another specialty. Les Ruchers de Bonnechère tend hives and make pottery only 12 km away at St. Michel l'Observatoire. Essential oils made from lavender and other aromatic plants are used for the bath, massage, and medicinal purposes. For mushrooms, you can do no better than Isabelle Baldaccini's selection.

Her husband grows them in an abandoned railway tunnel (see p. 64).

Shops dot the narrow, winding streets. Galleries and craft studios pop up in unexpected places. Le Noën (10 Avenue Fontauris) stands out as a boutique that sells luxury-quality leather items. Philippe Le Noën worked at Hermès and Louis Vuitton and now creates bags, wallets, and belts out of exceptional skins in his own workshop.

Although the area boasts 300 days of sunshine each year, my visits always coincide with one of the others. Cafés along the market's edge extend their awnings. Customers sip coffee (or stronger drinks) to fortify themselves as rain patters overhead. Even on a damp day, this market bustles with activity. Hardy vendors and shoppers troop out for their weekly routine. Whatever the weather, the Forcalquier market and its surroundings will put you in a sunny mood.

Forcalquier also hosts a small farmers' market on Thursday from 3 to 7 p.m. in Place Martial Sicard.

Rossano and Isabelle Baldaccini, Mushroom Farmers

One of the most unusual farms is inside an abandoned railway tunnel. The train that had transported cargo to and from Forcalquier stopped operating in 1960. Rossano Baldaccini carries a flashlight as we enter the old tunnel. Mushrooms protrude from the walls and dangle from the ceiling. It is a bizarre sight of odd-colored and strangely shaped life-forms.

Rosanno grows shiitake, *pleurote,* shimeji, *pied bleu,* and white button *champignons de Paris,* which he cleverly renamed "Par'ici" since they're not grown in Paris. He also cultivates *endivettes,* slender white shoots that grow after the stem has been cut. The absence of light prevents the leaves from turning green. Their pale color and delicate crunch add an unusual flair to salads.

His growing method has long-standing precedent. Farmers grew mushrooms in abandoned quarries underneath Paris (*champignons de Paris*) before the construction of the Métro. A handful of Parisian farmers still cultivate them in the catacombs. Temperature, humidity, and controlled light conditions are constant, so seasonality isn't an issue. Rossano halts production for a month each year to scrub and disinfect the tunnel.

Isabelle sells the mushrooms and *endivettes* at the Forcalquier and Manosque markets. Their division of labor suits them: A quiet man, Rossano prefers the solitude of the tunnel and the music that he pipes in, while Isabelle welcomes the social interaction at markets. The farm is not open to the public for reasons of hygiene, but the mushrooms are available for all to enjoy if you get to the markets before the supply runs out. Even the simplest preparation releases a sublime, earthy flavor—toss in olive oil, sprinkle with herbs, and spread atop a bowl of pasta.

· OTHER MONDAY MARKETS ·

Lauris

· SMALL PROVENÇAL MARKET ·

WHEN: *Monday morning*

WHERE: *Place Joseph Garnier*

ARKETS IN PROVENCE range in size from large extravaganzas that attract people from far and wide, as in Aix-en-Provence, to medium-sized village markets, such as Lourmarin, that draw locals and tourists in the vicinity, to very small markets that serve a particular village. Lauris is one of the latter. Only a few vendors attend, but the quality is decent, and there's enough to satisfy residents' needs. It takes only a few minutes to mosey among the stands. Or stay longer to chat with vendors and observe how weekly markets animate the rhythm of village life.

Locals know the fishmonger; some make his truck their first stop. Others head straight to the butcher for quail, pigeon, duck, or rabbit. The aroma of sizzling spareribs and rotisserie chicken tempts a few to spare the fuss of cooking and buy a ready-made meal.

It's easy to park and stock up on picnic food before getting on with the day. A nearby attraction is Le Jardin Conservatoire des

Plantes Tinctoriales, a botanical garden dedicated to plants from which natural dyes are extracted. It's located on the terraces of the Lauris castle with views overlooking the Durance valley.

Tourist Offices

Provence is the second most popular tourist destination in France, attracting over 30 million visitors each year. I don't usually visit tourist offices when I travel elsewhere, but I make them my first stop in Provence to pick up a local map and learn about activities and events. The staff speaks English, and the offices are generally well stocked with useful resources.

Located in the center of most towns and villages, the Office de Tourisme is identifiable by the "i" sign. Follow it to navigate to the market, because it's usually close. Offices in Aix-en-Provence, Arles, Avignon, Apt, L'Isle-sur-la-Sorgue, Carpentras, La Tour d'Aigues, and Vaison-la-Romaine are tasked with serving a wider region and do it well. Several have exhibition space and a gift shop showcasing local products.

Nîmes

❧ FLEA AND ANTIQUES MARKET ❧

WHEN: *Monday morning*

WHERE: *Allées Jaurès*

THE NÎMES *BROCANTE* (flea and antiques market) is advertised as being open all day, but savvy shoppers arrive about 8 a.m. to sift through a variety of household and farm items—tools, furniture, linens, clothing, glassware, silverware, and ceramics. Occasionally one can find *santons*. Many of the roughly 80 vendors start packing up at noon. The market's setting on the west side of town is not especially interesting, but stroll down the main avenue to Les Jardins de la Fontaine. These lovely gardens and the impressive Roman ruins in Nîmes will leave you with a very different impression of the town's past and present glory.

On Sunday morning there is a flea market in the parking lot by the football stadium, Stade des Costières, but the Monday *brocante* is more interesting. For a description of Les Halles de Nîmes, the covered food market, see p. 213.

Saint-Didier

·SMALL PROVENÇAL MARKET·

WHEN: *Monday morning*

WHERE: *Village center*

SAINT-DIDIER is a pretty village between Carpentras and Venasque. Every Monday morning the otherwise unremarkable main road and parking lot behind town hall are transformed into a colorful marketplace. The usual offerings can be found, from table linens and handbags to fresh produce, honey, cheese, and wine. Trimmed sycamores and orderly rows of stalls frame a view of the church's bell tower. Birdsong blends with the chimes in a natural harmony. You might decide to linger; the serenity of Saint-Didier can be seductive.

Local Cheese

Goat cheeses are often sold directly by farmers at the markets. The best are available from spring through autumn, during milking season. The character of the cheese varies by age, ranging from one or two days old to over a week. The youngest are described as fresh and the oldest as dry, with several gradations in between. Fresh goat cheese has a high water content. The cheese shrinks as it dries, which intensifies the flavor and changes the consistency from soft and buttery to hard and crumbly. It's not that one is better than the other, but everyone has a preference. That's why a typical Provençal cheese plate consists of one fresh goat cheese, one medium, and one aged. Variations include cheeses that are rolled in herbs, or topped with minced shallots, garlic, or red pepper flakes. Thimble-sized cheeses are perfect for popping in the mouth whole.

Banon is a prized specialty cheese of Provence with a nutty, earthy aroma. Each round is wrapped in chestnut leaves—originally a method for preserving them through the winter—and tied into a small brown bundle with a label bearing the AOC (or AOP) emblem. Banon is the only Provençal cheese that has been awarded an AOC designation. The type of goat, where the animals pasture, and other details about production are tightly regulated. The flavor is so addictive as to lend credibility to the legend that the Roman emperor Antoninus Pius died of indigestion from having eaten too much of it.

Brousse du Rove is a fresh goat cheese, so soft and runny that it's often sold in a cone-shaped wrapper. It comes from Le Rove, a village west of Marseille near the Mediterranean coast. Other cheeses worthy of mention come from areas close to Provence. *Picodon,* from the Drôme, has a slight kick (the name means "spicy" in the Provençal language). *Pélardon,* a soft-ripened goat cheese, comes from goats grazing in the Cévennes range of Languedoc-Roussillon.

Tuesday

· MARKETS ·

Best

Cucuron *(traditional Provençal market)*

Gordes *(traditional Provençal market)*

La Tour d'Aigues *(traditional Provençal market)*

Saint-Saturnin-lès-Apt *(traditional Provençal market)*

Tarascon *(traditional Provençal market)*

Vaison-la-Romaine *(traditional Provençal market)*

Aix-en-Provence *(traditional Provençal market)*, see p. 151

Avignon *(covered market)*, see p. 161

Velleron *(farmers' market)*, see p. 133

Others

Apt *(farmers' market)*

Beaumes-de-Venise *(traditional Provençal market)*

Lourmarin *(farmers' market)*

Saint-Rémy de Provence *(craft market)*

Nîmes *(covered market)*, see p. 213

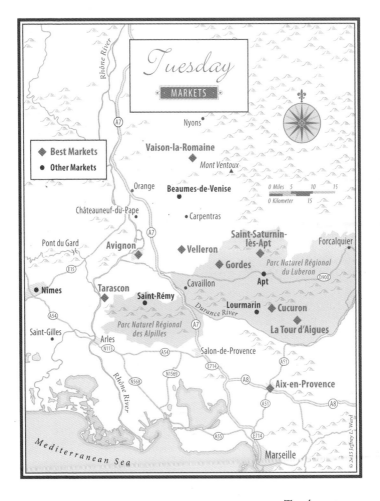

Best Markets

Other Markets

Tuesday
MARKETS

Rhône River

A7

Nyons

Vaison-la-Romaine

Mont Ventoux

Orange

Beaumes-de-Venise

Châteauneuf-du-Pape

Carpentras

A7

Saint-Saturnin-
lès-Apt

Pont du Gard

Avignon

Velleron

Forcalquier

E15

Gordes

Parc Naturel Régional
du Luberon

D900

Nîmes

Tarascon

Saint-Rémy

Cavaillon

Apt

Lourmarin

Cucuron

Durance River

Parc Naturel Régional
des Alpilles

A7

La Tour d'Aigues

Saint-Gilles

Arles

N113

A54

Salon-de-Provence

A51

N568

N1569

E714

A8

A55

E714

Aix-en-Provence

A51

A8

Marseille

Mediterranean Sea

0 Miles 5 10 15
0 Kilometer 15

© 2015 Jeffrey L. Ward

Cucuron

WHEN: *Tuesday morning*

WHERE: *Place de l'Étang in village center*

OFFICE DE TOURISME: *Cours Pourrières,
84160 Cucuron. Tel: 04.90.77.28.37. www.cucuron-luberon.com*

CUCURON IS ONE OF the sweetest markets in Provence. The market owes its charm to the storybook setting next to a large basin, which is actually a spring-fed pool. The *bassin de l'Étang* dates to the early 14th century and is bordered by plane trees over 200 years old. They seem to be reaching across the water to clasp leafy hands. Reflections of the mottled trunks ripple on the water's surface, doubling their beauty and giving the impression that one has landed in an enchanted garden. Certainly there's magic in the air, even—or perhaps especially—when the mistral races around the stalls like an invisible trickster.

Legend has it that the village got its name from Julius Caesar, who asked *"Cur currunt?"* (Why do they run?) when villagers scattered upon his arrival. Nowadays it's a gathering spot and a popular location site for films, such as *A Good Year,* based on the Peter Mayle novel, and *Le Hussard sur le Toit* (*The Horseman on the Roof*), based on the novel by Jean Giono.

The market is relatively small, but its high quality is on a par with its setting. Stands line three sides of the basin and continue up the road at the far end. Most Provençal markets sprawl along narrow, winding streets, making it impossible to step back and take in the total effect. But the layout of Cucuron's market encourages drinking in the view in one long, delicious swallow.

A fruit and vegetable seller does a brisk business. Carrots marked *bio* (organic) with soil clinging to them are piled in a bin next to well-scrubbed ones at a lower price. Sweet Cavaillon melons pair nicely with cured ham. Henri Sabatier sells apricots and cherries that he picked at his orchard. When he learns that I'm American, he shows me pictures of his vintage Mustang and TransAm. They're sleek, but his perfectly ripened apricots impress me more. Thierry Perez sells cheeses that he and Sophie make at their goat farm in Peypin d'Aigues. Some are sprinkled with ash, garlic, savory, or thyme. *Apiculteurs* Florence and Thierry Rumeau-Schurch sell honeys that are naturally scented with rosemary, chestnut flower, and other wild plants. They also make a syrup with thyme and honey. Combine it with white wine for an *apéritif,* or drizzle it atop fruits and crêpes. Les Confitures de Caroline has homemade jams and vinegars.

The butcher's case is stocked with thick marbled cuts of beef and chunks of lamb on skewers. Pork ribs and chicken have been roasting to a juicy golden brown. At *poissonerie* Poi, tuna and swordfish are arrayed on ice next to oysters and shrimp. Artichoke salad, *céleri rémoulade,* and chickpea salad look tempting. Cured ham is expertly sliced at a stand that displays a Spanish flag with a bull at the center.

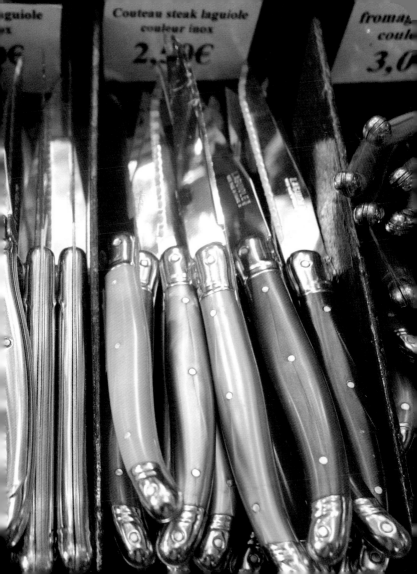

Interspersed with the food stands are vendors selling soaps, lavender oils, table linens, market baskets, and jewelry. Kitchen gadgets make good souvenirs: cheese knives, jam spreaders, honey dippers, and spoons in crooked shapes that rest easily atop jars. Local potters display earthenware bowls. Ceramic dishes at other stands delight with their rainbow of colors, but they're not locally made.

I'm laden with sacks of purchases, but it's not a burden to carry them as I explore the twisty streets of Cucuron, which has been designated one of the Most Beautiful Villages of France with its medieval walls, gurgling fountains, a clock tower that was erected in 1541, and the remains of a dungeon. From a high perch, you might see Cézanne's beloved Mont Sainte-Victoire in the distance.

I meander back down the narrow streets and return once more to the market. Art students with sketchpads have set up chairs and are trying to capture the scene, yet its shimmering beauty eludes even their most talented efforts.

Gordes

WHEN: *Tuesday morning*

WHERE: *Village center*

OFFICE DE TOURISME: *Le Château, 84220 Gordes.*
Tel: 04.90.72.02.75. www.gordes-village.com

ᕈERCHED ATOP A ROCKY CLIFF, Gordes is one of the most picturesque villages in Provence. Bleached morning light illuminates the village like a religious painting. Its silhouette might look familiar, since it was featured in *A Good Year,* with Russell Crowe and Marion Cotillard, and other movies. The village's dramatic setting makes it a popular location for film crews and wealthy villas.

The local economy flourished in the 18th and early 19th centuries with silk production, tanning, and shoemaking. After a long period of decay, the village has been revitalized as a tourist destination. The market is delightful though geared more to tourists and part-time residents than to villagers.

Colorful stalls wrap around the base of the medieval *château* like a beaded necklace around a weathered neck. Chirping toy cicadas seem to sing louder as the day heats up. Oil paintings, watercolors, and photographs do a good job of capturing the local landscape. Fragrant soaps, *herbes de Provence* in ceramic grinders, and truffled seasoning salts make nice gifts. Provençal tablecloths and scarves hang from several stalls, fluttering like the flags of proud nations.

A man whistles as he slices onions and potatoes and places them on the grill next to lamb sausages. Tantalizing smells fill the market by midmorning. A stand offers *caillette aux herbes* (pork with spinach or chard leaves, seasoned with garlic and herbs). Chunks of potatoes glistening with olive oil and tomatoes stuffed with ground beef (*tomate farcie*) are Provençal favorites. A table spread with fruits and vegetables reminds visitors that the surrounding farmland is France's food basket. Not everything sold here, however, is from the region. The *foie gras* was made in southwest France; the *jambon* comes from Haute Savoie. But most shoppers are not making fine distinctions about how local the sources are. One group buys cheese, bread, salami, olives, and wine for a picnic under the wall of the castle in nearby Murs.

The village is so visually arresting that it shouldn't be missed. Labyrinthine streets thread under vaulted passageways. A castle with rounded towers served as a fortified defense during the religious wars. Church bells sound at noon, but no one seems harried as morning dissolves into afternoon. Even the policeman directing traffic near the statue of war heroes yawns as motorists file into town.

As you leave Gordes, take another look at its jagged profile, which might be best appreciated from a slight distance as the afternoon sun casts a honeyed glow. You may wish to explore the marvelous Abbaye de Sénanque, about 4 km from Gordes. The 12th-century monastery is still an active community of Cister-

cian monks. Their lavender fields make a breathtaking sight in summer. At Village des Bories, igloo-shaped huts of unmortared stone served as places to store farm equipment and sometimes give shelter to farmers working their fields. They make a curious sight. A short side trip to the village of Murs will thrill you with ancient trees and buildings fashioned from local sandstone.

La Tour d'Aigues

❧ TRADITIONAL PROVENÇAL MARKET ❧

WHEN: *Tuesday morning*

WHERE: *In front of the castle on Place Jean Jaurès*

OFFICE DE TOURISME: *Le Château, 84240 La Tour d'Aigues.
Tel: 04.90.07.50.29. www.luberoncotesud.com*

THE CASTLE IN LA TOUR D'AIGUES was once considered the most architecturally ambitious in Provence. Records as far back as 1039 make reference to a *château*. The original structure was probably simple and spare, but in the mid-1500s it was transformed by the addition of two large square towers and a gateway in the form of a triumphal arch. The architecture was inspired by the lavish castles in Île de France, such as Pierre Lescot's Cour Carrée in the Louvre palace. Many notable figures passed through the impressive gate of the *château* in La Tour d'Aigues, once heralded as the finest example of Renaissance architecture in the land.

In 1792, a revolutionary mob attacked the castle. A fire blazed for five days and nights, after which the remains were plundered. The site was neglected for nearly a century, and its crumbling *façade* deteriorated. The *château* was declared a historic monument, and funds are helping restore the castle little by little. Outdoor festivals, concerts, and other cultural events are held here.

The market caters to local residents and serves their basic needs:

clothing, shoes, kitchen gadgets, and food at reasonable prices. Stands with fish, meat, furniture, jewelry, eggs, vegetables, and mattresses follow one after another in no apparent order. A vegetable seller sprays heads of lettuce to keep them fresh even as the late-morning sun threatens to wilt them. Olives infuse the air with a tangy aroma which, in only a few steps, is replaced by sweet-smelling lavender.

A nattily clad man sells *sirop Châtaigne* (chestnut syrup). He suggests mixing it with white wine for an *apéritif.* Warm paella, Asian noodles, and rotisserie chicken are tempting as easy, yet satisfying, lunches. Dessert can be just as convenient if you buy a handful of biscuits flavored with orange blossom or anise.

As closing time approaches, a woman selling wine passes around glasses for friends. Another shares slices of quiche. The Provençal character is on display in their good-natured banter and generous exchange. A friendly warmth flows through this market, as unimpeded as the breeze that courses through the spaces between the castle's remaining walls.

La Tour d'Aigues also hosts a farmers' market on Thursday morning from May through September at the Place du Monument.

What *is* Provence?

The question vexed me when I began my research. I had assumed it was a well-defined territory but rarely saw an area labeled as such on maps. The harder I tried to pinpoint Provence, the more elusive it seemed. The name comes from *provincia*—a province of the Roman Empire—and is part of PACA (Provence–Alpes–Côte d'Azur), a region comprising six *départements*. But there is no single administrative body, and its geographical boundaries are murky. I came to understand that there is no consensus on what and where Provence is, exactly.

Provence is more a culture than a clearly defined area. Locals are proud to be *Provençaux*. It's a treasured part of their identity. It is a heritage that was shaped by the Romans and a mind-set that attaches great importance to quality of life, outdoor living, local foods, wines, and traditions.

If you find yourself confused by the geography while planning a trip to Provence, you're not alone. Even the locals are unable to agree on its physical outline, although they have a ready reply for where the *heart* of Provence lies: wherever *they* are living.

Saint-Saturnin-lès-Apt

❖ SMALL PROVENÇAL MARKET ❖

WHEN: *Tuesday morning*

WHERE: *Village center*

Saint-Saturnin-lès-Apt is a quiet village nestled on a hill in the Vaucluse countryside. The village is in the shadow of better-known Roussillon and Apt, which makes the pleasure of discovering it even sweeter. Few tourists come here, and that contributes to its rustic charm. Built on a slope that faces south toward the Luberon, the medieval village has narrow streets, red-tiled roofs, and wooden shutters painted periwinkle blue and avocado green. Ornately carved doors and other architectural flourishes add interest to several homes along Rue de la République.

Villagers make their rounds early, filling straw baskets with a week's worth of provisions while catching up on village news. It takes only a few minutes to traverse this market, but for the locals it becomes an extended social ritual. Large burlap sacks bulge with herbs and spices. Fresh eggs and cherries come from local farms and orchards. A fishmonger filets the silvery catch according to customers' requests. *Poulet rôti* and couscous might appeal to those who crave a ready-made meal.

Goat cheeses in the shape of corks (*bouchons*) are the perfect bite-size for appetizers. An *apiculteur* will be happy to give you a taste of local honeys. Chestnut honey has an intense flavor with a slightly bitter aftertaste; lavender is more fragrant and floral; rosemary is light and refined. My favorite is *garrigue,* made by bees that have been feeding on the local rosemary, thyme, and savory.

In the main square, there's a statue of a man kneeling. At first glance he seems to be a player studying his next move in a game

of *pétanque* (also called *boules*). A closer look reveals that it isn't a ball he's holding but a large black truffle. This replica of Joseph Talon celebrates his development of truffle cultivation, or truffi-culture. Talon was born in 1793 in the hamlet of Croagnes in Saint-Saturnin-lès-Apt. He observed that truffles were growing on the roots of oak trees on his farm, so he gathered acorns from those trees and sowed them in his fields. About ten years later, he unearthed a bounty of truffles clinging to the roots of young oak trees. He sold the truffles, becoming rich and the envy of his neighbors. He told no one his secret, but someone spied on him. Soon farmers were asking Talon for "truffle oaks," and he began selling seedlings inoculated with the fungi. Joseph Talon's ingenuity made him a fortune, and it inspired this statue in his honor. Truffles are still harvested in the oak-covered hills nearby. In winter, a vendor sets up a table near Talon's statue. He's happy to sell you oak seedlings that might have descended from Talon's plantation.

Behind the village, steps lead up to ruins of a castle and views of the Luberon valley. There's a restored windmill and a man-made lake that collects water from the Vaucluse plateau. Or simply settle in a chair at one of the cafés in Saint-Saturnin-lès-Apt and relax with an afternoon *pastis* as the Provençal sun casts long and lazy shadows. If you happen to visit in July, note that the village hosts a flea market on Bastille Day (July 14).

Tarascon

WHEN: *Tuesday morning*

WHERE: *Cours Aristide Briand, Avenue de la République, Rue des Halles, and Place de Verdun*

OFFICE DE TOURISME: *Avenue de la République, 13150 Tarascon. Tel: 04.90.91.03.52.*
www.tourisme@tarascon.org

TARASCON LIES ALONG the Rhône River's western bank, roughly midway between Avignon and Arles. It is well located for excursions to those cities, as well as to villages throughout the Alpilles and the Camargue. Tarascon is linked to colorful legends. An amphibious monster known as the Tarasque terrorized river traffic until he was tamed by Saint Martha and butchered by the townspeople. The Tarasque lives on in local traditions, such as baked goods designed like a ferocious mouth. Another legendary local, Tartarin de Tarascon, is a plump, middle-aged character created by Alphonse Daudet. The city hosts a festival the last weekend in June to celebrate the vanquishing of the Tarasque and commemorate the Tartarin tales.

On market day, the best food stands are in the heart of the old city. Frédéric and Sandrine Gautier sell fresh olives and tapenades. *Cassées fenouil,* olives that are crushed and then sprinkled with fennel, and black olives from Nyons are two of my favorites. *Tellines,* small clams with golden-gray shells, are a local delicacy. Rinse them well, then toss them in a pan with olive oil, garlic, a splash of white wine, and chopped parsley for a delicious topping to pasta that takes only minutes to prepare. You can find *tellines* and other shellfish at the stand Graulou Coquillage, where a woman sells her husband's catch. She'll give you recipes if you ask and show photos of her husband wading in his high rubber boots.

In spring, the perfume of *gariguette* strawberries at Lafaye

Christian's stand can be detected from afar. *Apiculteur* Jean-Paul Barbesier sells local honeys. Cheeses at Le Mas du Trident include *brousse,* a fresh and soft ricotta-style cheese similar to the Corsican *brocciu* cheese. The *tomme de brébis* (a firm sheep's-milk cheese) pairs nicely with a white wine from Les Baux. The vendor kindly makes the effort to explain in English that he sells both goat and sheep cheese—which, to my embarrassment, I initially misunderstand as "cheap" cheese. I chalk it up as part of the fun.

Tarascon has some notable shops. Boulangerie Bio Les 7 Épis (2 Rue Esquiros in Place Gonthier) sells organic breads, such as *fougasse Provençale* made with olives, and the well-named *pain de joie* with spelt, dried fruits, and nuts. *Pâtisserie-chocolatier* La Tarasque, on Rue des Halles, decorates cakes to look like the Tarasque monster and sweets that honor Tartarin. Anyone interested in textiles and design will enjoy a visit to the Souleiado shop at 39 Rue Charles-Deméry. Souleiado has twenty boutiques in Provence, but the company's headquarters and museum are in Tarascon. The vivid colors and timeless designs of its *Indienne* fabrics make a terrific souvenir and can be purchased in the boutique. *Souleiado* is a Provençal word that refers to the moment when the rain ends and the sky brightens again. The museum is also worth a visit for exhibits of print blocks, textile designs, and traditional Provençal clothing.

Tarascon has a weekly flea market on Sunday morning at the Intermarché parking lot at ZAC du Roubian. There's a lot of junk, but it holds the promise of unexpected treasure. The city also hosts holiday markets in November and December.

Vaison-la-Romaine

WHEN: *Tuesday morning*

WHERE: *Town center*

OFFICE DE TOURISME: *Place du Chanoine Sautel,
84110 Vaison-la-Romaine. Tel: 04.90.36.02.11.
www.vaison-ventoux-tourisme.com*

OVER 2,000 YEARS AGO, Roman legionnaires built Vaison into one of the most prosperous cities in Provence. Ruins give clues about life at that time: lavish homes, shopping districts, public baths, private gardens, and a large theater. Archaeologists continue to excavate, giving this town the distinction of being the largest archaeological site in France open to the public.

But the main draw for many visitors is Vaison's weekly market. Pope Sixtus IV granted a market license in 1483; in 1532, Pope Clement VII stipulated that the market be held every Tuesday, and the tradition has continued. It attracts about 450 vendors in the height of the season. The market is concentrated along Avenue Général de Gaulle and Cours Taulignan, but it spills into side streets and squares. A pleasant starting point is Place Montfort in the heart of the modern town, where a large public square was recently paved and renovated. On market days it fills with vendors.

Local goat-cheese producers bring fresh and aged *chèvres.*

Stands overflow with tangled green beans, frizzy lettuces, and dimpled peppers. Wooden crates with white and purple asparagus empty fast. Trout, halibut, and scorpion fish lie across beds of ice at the fishmongers. Signs explain where each variety was caught. Pink Himalayan salt, coarse gray sea salt, and flaky *fleur de sel* are mounded high at Les Senteurs de Vaison. You can buy loose leaves for brewing *tisanes* such as hibiscus, apricot, lavender, and rose.

Monsieur Robert makes jams and nectars from fruits he cultivates at his farm, Le Moulin des Rosières in Mondragon. They burst with the intense flavor of strawberries, plums, and peaches. His tomatoes are also popular among the locals, who swing by his stand early in the day before he sells out. Nos Saveurs Provençales is another producer of high-quality jams and spreads. The *confit d'olives noires,* deep black and rich in flavor, goes down smoothly. L'Or Rouge des 3 Rivières has pure saffron and saffron-related products. Christine Tracol sells local honey. Hungry shoppers form a line at the Pizza Mumu truck, where the thin crust and light tomato sauce serve as a base for anchovy and black olive toppings.

A small section devoted to local farmers is at Espace Culturel in Place François Cevert. (On Saturday morning, Vaison holds a slightly larger farmers' market.) A man and his young daughter peer into boxes filled with squawking chickens. They choose one and hand over a few euros, buying it for the eggs.

Provençal pottery, market baskets, and table linens make long-lasting mementos, as do olive-wood utensils and cutting boards, even though most are from Spain or Tunisia. Linen clothing comes in comfortable designs. Prices are reasonable, and the items hold up at least a season.

The market sights are colorful and compelling, but raise your eyes once in a while to take in the long view. The remains of a feudal castle atop a hill mark the medieval town where villagers fled for protection from invaders. It offers panoramic views of modern Vaison, and a walk there might evoke the imagined sounds of previous generations trading goods.

Don't leave Vaison without visiting its outstanding shops. Cheesemonger Josiane Déal won the Meilleur Ouvrier de France award—the highest distinction conferred upon specialists—for her cheese shop Lou Canestéou (10 Rue Raspail). At Gargantua butcher shop and delicatessen (44 Cours Taulignan), Gilles Digle makes his own sausages, perfectly roasted ham, and *Pontias saucisson* with olives.

End any excursion to Vaison on a high note by visiting Peyrerol chocolate shop (7 Cours Henri Fabre) for some of the finest chocolates in the land. Gilles Peyrerol was born into the trade as the son of a *chocolatier* and *pâtissier*. His creativity extends beyond the recipes: One Mother's Day he made chocolates in the shape of Louis Vuitton handbags, and one summer he created cakes in the shape of flip–flops.

· OTHER TUESDAY MARKETS ·

Apt

· FARMERS' MARKET ·

WHEN: *Tuesday morning*

WHERE: *Cours Lauze de Perret*

APT IS KNOWN FOR its large Saturday market with a wide range of offerings (see p. 227), but locals know that the *marché paysan* (farmers' market) on Tuesday is another opportunity to buy high-quality fresh produce at reasonable prices. Only local producers are permitted to sell at this market, and farming must be their main vocation.

Large heads of lettuce are so recently picked that they glisten with morning dew. Lucette Guglielmino sells cherries that she and her husband, Patrick, grow on their farm in Bonnieux. Lucette is active in the Bienvenue à la Ferme program, which means she welcomes visitors to her farm. You might also find at her stand copies of a cookbook containing recipes contributed by farmers who attend this market. Each dish features local ingredients, such as *velouté potimarron* and *beignets de fleurs de courgettes*. Le Suif sells thimble-size cheeses dusted with ground herbs, and larger rounds of goat cheese. Another farmer offers samples of his wines. It may take only 15 minutes to make the rounds of this market, but it won't take long to observe the tight social bonds and the strong ties that bind the people to the land.

Jean-Luc Danneyrolles,
Seed Saver

When he began farming, Jean-Luc sold flowers and vegetables at the markets. "Gastronomy is in my blood and my heart," he says, adding by way of explanation that he was born near Lyon. He worked with chefs such as Alain Ducasse and Reine Sammut, experimenting with varieties that they incorporated into their cooking. In the 1990s he started swapping seeds with other collectors, and his interests evolved into a passion for preserving biodiversity.

Le Potager d'un Curieux (the Garden of a Curious Man) is divided into distinct gardens. Orderly rows of lettuce build in color intensity from chartreuse to flame red. A circle of mixed lettuces at the center seems radically untamed by comparison and resolves the design into a balanced harmony. The tomato garden features 65 varieties, bordered by flowers that keep insects away. A garden of edible flowers is dedicated to the conservation of old and rare species. All the plants are organic and well labeled.

Danneyrolles has a wiry build and intense eyes. He thoughtfully nudges a stone aside when he says, "To gar-

den is to write on the soil." Eating well doesn't require a lot of land, but instead lots of discipline, patience, and, most important, good seeds. The gardens serve as a laboratory for experimentation and seed preservation, as a food source for the volunteers who work the land, and as a showroom so that visitors can see choices before selecting seeds. The produce is not sold to the public, but the seeds are.

Danneyrolles is building a nonprofit organization to disseminate his environmental philosophy and seed-conservation techniques. Volunteers from around the world come to work at Le Potager d'un Curieux. "I was considered suspect when I started collecting seeds," he says. "People didn't know what to make of me." But now, 30 years later, the seeds that he sowed are taking root with many farmers who share his sense of urgency.

Le Potager d'un Curieux welcomes visitors. A treehouse and painted signs add whimsy to the gardens. But make no mistake, the main objective is serious. Seeds can be purchased at the shop. It is located about 5 minutes outside of Saignon and 10 minutes from Apt at La Molière, 84400 Saignon. Route yourself to Saignon and then follow signs to Le Potager d'un Curieux. (www.lepotager duncurieux.org).

Beaumes-de-Venise

❧ · SMALL PROVENÇAL MARKET · ❧

WHEN: *Tuesday morning*

WHERE: *Cours Jean Jaurès*

NARROW STREETS, shaded squares, and weathered fountains give this village charm. But the best gift of all was from the ancient Greeks, who brought the Muscat grape. Hillsides are planted with the vines. Muscat de Beaumes-de-Venise ranks among France's best sweet white wines and earned the commune the privilege of its own appellation. The local Côtes du Rhône Villages red wines are also quite good. Local olive oils are almost as important as the wines. Moulin Balméenne offers tastes at its shop.

Peaches, plums, cherries, and melons pair well with the Muscat wine. Flowers, soaps, breads, herbs, and olives are plentiful. Several restaurants and cafés offer an opportunity to turn the outing into a social occasion.

Beaumes-de-Venise is only 8 km north of Carpentras, but it feels a world apart with its rustic character and hiking trails. The village rises up to sandstone cliffs that run along the foothills of the Dentelles de Montmirail. *Beaume* means grotto or cave, and the cliffs are filled with them. At one time many were inhabited. The chapel of Notre Dame d'Aubune is notable for its Romanesque architecture and elegant bell tower. For a picturesque stroll, park there and follow the path into the village.

Lourmarin

⟨ EVENING FARMERS' MARKET ⟩

WHEN: *Tuesday evening, May through October, 5:30–8:30 p.m.*

WHERE: *Agricultural cooperative along Route D943*

*A*S IF LOURMARIN'S LARGE Friday morning market weren't enough to keep the larders in this village well stocked (see p. 205), there's also a farmers' market on Tuesday evening during the growing season. The evening market is devoted to local *producteurs*. About 25 vendors sell vegetables and fruits, juices, breads, jams, cheeses, meats, and flowers near an old loading dock at the village's former agricultural cooperative. Local wines and beers are sold by the glass.

The highlight is a cooking demonstration that features a different chef each week who composes a menu based on seasonal ingredients. Some are culinary celebrities, such as Reine Sammut, Eric Sapet, Édouard Loubet, and others who work in the best kitchens in and around Lourmarin. They seem to enjoy the evening's festivities as much as everyone else as they roll up their sleeves and take command of the whisk and spatula. Samples are passed out to a hungry crowd, and recipes are posted on the Internet.

108 ❊ MARKETS OF PROVENCE

Saint-Rémy-de-Provence

WHEN: *Tuesday evening, 7 p.m.–midnight,
from July through mid-September*

WHERE: *Place de la Mairie and Avenue de la Résistance*

GRAND *ALLÉES* of plane trees and fields of red poppies bring to mind paintings of Provence. It's awe-inspiring to come upon a scene so familiar that it feels as if you're looking at it through Vincent van Gogh's eyes. The colors and forms of the Provençal landscape have long attracted artists, and they still do. Tuesday evening in summer, artisans sell ceramics, textiles, jewelry, hats, soaps, glassware, and leather goods. Everything must be handmade and sold by the artists themselves. Another opportunity to see local art is the "Route des Artistes" event when painters, sculptors, and photographers display their work around Saint-Rémy on five Sundays, generally once each in May, June, August, September, and October. Whether or not you find something that you want to bring home, strolling these specialty markets is a way of connecting with the town's storied artistic past and its equally promising future.

The Market Day

Six or seven days a week, vendors load up their vans at 5 a.m. and drive, sometimes a considerable distance, to market. In winter it's pitch-dark as a procession of *camionnettes* streams into a village. Starting around 6 a.m., headlights illuminate the market area as vehicles squeeze between plane trees. Each market has regular merchants who take their usual spots, having prepaid a yearly fee. Roving merchants are not guaranteed a space, so as soon as they arrive they track down the market's *placier*, whose job it is to manage this process.

There are often more vendors than available space. Each *placier* handles the process differently, but usually it's determined by a lottery system, by who arrives first, or by the *placier* favoring vendors he recognizes. The better known a merchant is to a *placier,* the more likely he or she is to get a good location. Hinges squeak, car doors slam, and tables get dragged into place. Fabric vendors arrange linens by similar dimensions. Fishmongers spread ice across trays and lay out the fresh catch. Oysters are sorted by size as swiftly as hands of poker. Rotisseries fire up; chickens are slid onto long metal skewers. Finishing touches dress up the displays—fennel fronds circle a bowl of olives, *saucisson* slices topple across cutting boards, and loaves of country bread form crisscross stacks.

Steam rises from mugs as vendors pour black coffee from carafes; a few sip wine to warm up. Several head to a café, where the proprietor prepares their breakfast order without needing to ask.

Around 8 a.m., the first shoppers arrive: locals who make a beeline for their favorite vendors. The last wave, generally tourists, starts about 9:30. The *placier* makes his rounds to check documentation (sellers are required to have permits) and collect money (the fee depends on the length of the stall).

Business begins to wind down at noon. By 1 p.m., transactions come to a halt. Vendors pack up bins and take down their stands. Narrow streets turn into elaborate jigsaw puzzles as merchants steer their vans between stalls and piles of empty crates. Gleaners show up, especially in the city markets, to retrieve discarded food.

Sanitation workers in green uniforms toss trash onto trucks, sweep up the debris, and hose down the streets. Their work, like the vendors', is executed with remarkable speed. Soon the streets and squares look pristine again. Café owners fill the space with tables and chairs, and streets reopen to traffic. And so the scene repeats day after day, year after year, in all kinds of weather.

Wednesday

· MARKETS ·

Best

Saint-Rémy *(traditional Provençal market)*

Sault *(traditional Provençal market)*

Velleron *(farmers' market)*

Avignon *(covered market)*, see p. 161

Others

Arles *(monthly flea/antiques market +
traditional Provençal market)*

Beaucaire *(flea/antiques market)*

Mouriès *(traditional Provençal market)*

Pernes-les-Fontaines *(farmers' market)*

Nîmes *(covered market)*, see p. 213

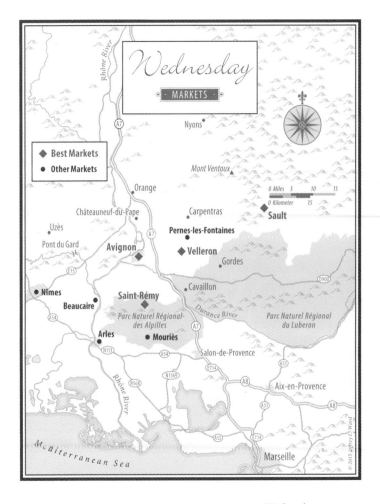

Wednesday

MARKETS

Nyons

Mont Ventoux

◆ Best Markets
● Other Markets

Orange

Carpentras

Sault

Châteauneuf-du-Pape

Pernes-les-Fontaines

Uzès

Pont du Gard

Avignon

◆ Velleron

Gordes

Nîmes

Cavaillon

Beaucaire

Saint-Rémy

Parc Naturel Régional
des Alpilles

Durance River

Parc Naturel Régional
du Luberon

Arles

Mouriès

Salon-de-Provence

Rhône River

Aix-en-Provence

Mediterranean Sea

Marseille

Rhône River

Saint-Rémy-de-Provence

⬥ TRADITIONAL PROVENÇAL MARKET ⬥

WHEN: *Wednesday morning*

WHERE: *Town center*

OFFICE DE TOURISME: *Place Jean Jaurès,*
13210 Saint-Rémy-de-Provence. Tel: 04.90.92.05.22.
www.saintremy-de-provence.com

SAINT-RÉMY is a relatively small town with an outsized reputation. One of the oldest towns in France, it flourished during the Roman era, was the birthplace of Nostradamus, and has been a magnet for artists inspired by the penetrating light. It is also a mecca for tourists, who flock here in summer for the market that swells to several hundred vendors and takes over the town center. Around every corner are new surprises: street performers, ancient fountains, specialty shops, and market stalls of all sorts.

A well-regarded olive vendor sets up in front of the town hall and attracts a line of eager customers. One Provençal specialty is *dents d'ail*—garlic that's been boiled and then marinated in olive oil and thyme. The cloves are crunchy and surprisingly mild. Locals pop them into their mouths like nuts. A seller of artisinal *saucissons* offers samples of dry-cured sausages made with wild boar and donkey. Sweet fragrances from lavender and vanilla soaps alternate with pungent cheeses and spices. Local honeys glisten like bottled sunshine. Signs marked *pays* indicate that the produce has come from the local countryside. Produce vendors display fresh asparagus, crisp radishes, and juicy strawberries in spring. In a few weeks their tables will be filled with cherries, Muscat grapes, figs, apricots, and melons. And always, always garlic; the local cuisine wouldn't be the same without it.

Fabien DuMont sells organic fruits and vegetables. La Charrette et le Fournil uses local grains in its breads, offering traditional loaves as well as variations studded with walnuts, olives, or apricots. Mélanie at La Fromagerie Roumanille originally bred cows for their meat, but now she specializes in organic cheese, ice cream, and yogurt. The cheeses at Fromages d'Hélène are well priced and of good quality, including goat cheese from the Drôme and *brocciu,* a slightly sweet Corsican cheese made with fresh sheep's milk. Nos Saveurs Provençales sells superb jams and *confit d'olives noires,* a black tapenade with intense flavor.

Antiques and flea-market items are at Place de la République. Rue Carnot is a hub for clothing and souvenirs. During the Renaissance, aristocratic families built mansions here. Several have been transformed into public spaces, such as the Musée des Alpilles.

Live jazz music drifts from Place Joseph Hilaire. It's the Gig Street quartet. You might not have expected to return from Saint-Rémy with a CD of American jazz, but you're unlikely to regret it. While you're in this quaint old square, step into *pâtisserie* Michel Marshall and *fromagerie* La Cave aux Fromages. A local specialty is the *brousse,* a fresh goat cheese.

Saint-Rémy has other notable shops with artisanal specialties, such as L'Épicerie du Calanquet at 8 Rue de la Commune, which sells high-quality olives, spreads, and olive oils that were pressed at a local mill. For chocolate lovers, Joël Durand at 3 Boulevard Victor Hugo is an essential stop. Le Petit Duc at 7 Boulevard Victor Hugo specializes in cookies. Lilamand Confiseur at 5 Avenue Albert Schweitzer has been making candied fruits and *calissons* by hand for five generations. They follow the recipe for *fruits confits* that Nostradamus referred to in his writings.

Adding to Saint-Rémy's appeal are art galleries, restaurants and cafés, and well-regarded museums. If you have a chance to linger after the market crowd has subsided, you'll be treated to an unimpeded view of Saint-Rémy. There are remnants of walls that once surrounded the town. It's said that the boulevards were built over moats.

You can't leave Saint-Rémy without visiting the Saint-Paul sanatorium, where Van Gogh painted some of his most celebrated works. A drive around the countryside of the Alpilles is certain to evoke the scenes and moods that he captured so memorably on canvas. The archaeological site at Glanum is only a kilometer from Saint-Rémy. A sound-and-light spectacle, Carrières de Lumières, is projected inside a stone quarry in nearby Les Baux-de-Provence. The theme changes every year. The village has been given over to tourist shops. Continue up the hill for panoramic views of the plains toward Arles and the Camargue.

Olives and Olive Oils

Olive trees have thrived on the southern slopes of the Alpilles and on the western slopes of Mont Ventoux since the Roman era. Most of the crop is used for olive oils (5 kilos of olives are needed to produce a liter of oil), but a few local varieties make outstanding table olives. The tastiest green olives are Lucques (firm and slightly sweet, grown primarily in Languedoc) and Picholines (elongated shape, grown in the Gard). The best black olives are Tanches—slightly wrinkled with a mild flavor, grown around Nyons and often called the Nyons olive. Tapenades, which are olives, capers, and anchovies puréed with olive oil into a smooth spread, originated in the south of France. I've heard them described as Provençal caviar.

Olives and tapenades are sold at the markets. Vendors often display them with flair and scoop them with ladles fashioned out of olive wood. Some vendors buy inventory ready-made from wholesalers. Others create the preparations themselves, and theirs are more flavorful. Request a sample to smell and taste for freshness. One of my favorites is *cassée fenouil*, broken olives marinated in brine and fennel. Olives are sold by weight, but if you want just a handful, ask for *"une bonne poignée, s'il vous plaît."* (continued)

Olive oils are not commonly found at the markets, since they're sensitive to temperature and light. An AOP designation on the label ensures quality since the producers are required to adhere to rigorous rules about growing methods and the preparation of the olives. A quality

olive oil will *se gratte dans la gorge* (catch in the throat). Depending on which varietals are used in the blend, the flavors range from floral to fruity to peppery. Olive oils that smell like fresh-cut grass perk up the flavor of vegetables; those with a hint of raw artichoke complement the local fish; a nutty flavor works with salads; peppery oils enhance the flavor of beef *carpaccio*. Oils from the southern region tend to have a brighter flavor than those made from the mild-flavored Tanche grown in the north, which makes the latter well suited for cooking.

Olive oil tasting can be as much fun as wine tasting, with similar complexity of flavors, and it's safer to drive afterward. Two places that I recommend are Château d'Estoublon, a working estate in Fontvieille with olive trees, vineyards, a castle, and a restaurant, and Moulin Castelas, an olive orchard and mill in Les Baux-de-Provence (see p. 141). If you purchase oils, keep them away from heat and light so they maintain peak flavor. Olive oils from Les Baux valley are some of the best in the world.

Chef Julien Drouot

A former electrical station on a road heading out of town hardly seems an inviting location for a restaurant, but customers are flocking to it. Julien and Claire Drouot won acclaim at Au Fils du Temps in Pernes-les-Fontaines, a cozy restaurant that continues to feature creative dishes under the direction of Chef Jerôme Campanelli. The Drouots wanted a bigger kitchen and more spacious dining, so they opened Maison Drouot. Julien cooks, while Claire serves and wows diners with her desserts and wine selection.

His kitchen philosophy boils down to three principles: "Use good products. Stick with the season. Make food that I want to eat." He describes his style as "modern Provençal," steering away from heavy sauces and highlighting natural flavors. "It's easy to do when you use local, fresh products." He gets lamb from the Alpilles, cheese from Mélanie Roumanille (who sells at several markets), bread from a local bakery, and olive oil from Calanquet in Saint-Rémy.

Before opening their restaurant, the Drouots explored the countryside and met with local producers. "Those relationships are essential to cooking with the best ingredients." My lunch started with red beet mousse, followed by seared tuna and, for dessert, a reinterpretation of the classic *tarte Tropézienne*.

Chef Drouot's advice for having good food experiences in Provence? "Avoid places with long menus because they're unlikely to do anything especially well." The same advice, he adds, applies to shopping at the markets: "Look for stands where there's not a lot of variety, but where they're focused on a few excellent items. Those are the producers, and their food will taste better. Their hands are probably dirty—always a good sign at the markets!"

Maison Drouot is at 1150 Route de Maillane, 13210 Saint-Rémy-de-Provence. Tel: 04.90.15.47.42. maison drouot.blogspot.com

Sault

❖ TRADITIONAL PROVENÇAL MARKET ❖

WHEN: *Wednesday morning*

WHERE: *Town center*

OFFICE DE TOURISME: *Avenue de la Promenade,
84390 Sault. Tel: 04.90.64.01.21. www.ventoux-sud.com*

*I*F YOU GLANCE AT A MAP, it might appear that Sault is too
far to warrant the travel time. But if ever the maxim applies
about enjoying the journey as much as the destination, it does
here. The route wends through mountains and plains beside fields
of wheat and lavender. In July and August the land is carpeted with
blue-purple blooms of lavender. On a clear day, the giant white-
capped Mont Ventoux is visible across the valley.

Sault is an old fortified village on a rocky promontory. The
market has existed since 1515. The Count of Sault decreed in 1546
that it always be on Wednesday. And it is still going strong almost
600 years later. Tourists turn up in summer, but locals keep this
market vital year-round, going not only to shop but also to catch
up on each other's news.

Périg Belloin sells superb goat cheeses, both fresh and aged.
Customers form a line, and his cheese case often empties long
before the market closes. Périg and his wife, Cathy, have a goat
farm in the hamlet of Saint-Jean-de-Sault (see p. 130). Bunches

of sunflowers, their perky yellow faces atop long thin necks, fill the arms of shoppers. Tomatoes are so plump that they barely fit in the palm. A grower from Mazan sells asparagus; another from Buis-les-Baronnies has olives, fruits, and juices. Lamb and pork from animals grazing the slopes of Mont Ventoux couldn't be tastier. Summer truffles with a pale interior can be shaved over a steaming plate of pasta or scrambled eggs to add a woodsy accent. If you hunger for something savory and ready-made, Le Petit Guillaume roasts perfectly golden chicken, duck, and quail.

Given its high elevation, Sault is in the heart of lavender country (see p. 16). (Sault hosts a lavender festival every August 15.) Harvesting goes from mid-July to mid-August. Farmers start with hand cutting and then shift to machines. Distilleries diffuse the fragrance, releasing the scent through their chimneys. Even the roadways give off a whiff from the trucks transporting distilled lavender. Several growers bring lavender bouquets, oils, sachets,

and soaps to the market. After the market, I recommend a visit to Arôma Plantes, a farm and distillery on Route de Ventoux that's open to the public. The gift shop has a wide selection of essential oils and other aromatic plant products.

Nougat is another local specialty. The André Boyer shop on Place de l'Europe is renowned for nougats with lavender honey and roasted almonds. It produces about 10 tons per year. The candies are popular at Christmas since nougats are two of the 13 desserts at the traditional holiday feast. Boyer also makes chewy *macarons,* crisp biscuits, and lavender honeys.

Petit-épautre has been grown around Sault for centuries. The ancient grain, similar to spelt, makes a nutritious accompaniment to vegetables, fish, or meat. It's also ground into flour and used in bread. A selection of local honeys (mostly lavender and thyme), spelt and spelt flour, chickpeas, dried herbs and spices, crafts, and souvenirs awaits anyone who explores Sault on market day.

Périg and Cathy Belloin,
Goat Farmers

At the market in Sault, I notice people lined up by a glass-fronted case of goat cheese. There is a slight but palpable sense of tension as customers wait their turn. Will the supply of *chèvre* last through their purchase? I hadn't realized at first that this stand belongs to Périg Belloin, whose farm I had planned to visit the next day.

Périg and Cathy Belloin tend about 55 goats in the hamlet of Saint-Jean-de-Sault. They are among the relatively rare breed of independent goat farmers. Most others sell their goats' milk to large dairies. The Belloins, however, handle the whole process themselves, from breeding and milking the goats to making and selling the cheeses. March to mid-November is peak season, since the goats are milked twice daily and graze on herbs, grasses, and scrubland that give the cheese its floral, earthy aroma.

Périg manages the herd with tender care. Unlike in industrialized dairies, where animals are kept indoors in cramped conditions, his goats roam the fields and woods. He brings them inside the barn only to be milked, in bad weather, and at night. He hand-feeds the kids with bottles to accustom them to human touch. I watch him milk the mature goats; they seem contented and at ease. He doesn't push them beyond their milking limits. They live up to 10 years, considerably longer than the 6-year average lifespan of goats at industrial dairies.

Périg and Cathy were urban dwellers before they chose to move to the country and learn the trade from scratch.

He takes care of the goats and sells at markets; she makes the cheese in a spotless facility next to the farm. It's only the two of them, along with several herding dogs. The goats must be milked twice daily for most of the year, which means that the Belloins can't venture far from their farm. Between tending the goats, making the cheese, and selling at markets, they work from dawn to dusk seven days a week.

"There's no room for either of us to get sick," Périg says. "But the reward is our quality of life." Cathy agrees that it's a life choice, adding a laugh as we stand ankle-deep in hay. "We live in a beautiful environment and have our independence." And, as I know from the previous morning at the Sault market, they also have a lot of appreciative customers.

The Périgs sell goat cheese at the Sault and Bédoin markets, and directly from their farm in Saint-Jean-de-Sault, 84390 Sault.

Velleron

WHEN: *From April to September, open every day except Sunday and bank holidays 6 p.m.–8 p.m.; from October to March, open Tuesday, Friday, and Saturday 4:30 p.m.–6:30 p.m.*

WHERE: *Parking lot at the edge of the village near route D938*

FOR THOSE WHO HUNGER to cook and eat the fresh bounty of Provence, the Velleron market is a dream come true. Local growers sell their harvest directly to shoppers at this exceptional *marché paysan*. It's the oldest farmers' market in the Vaucluse and unusual in being open as frequently as six evenings a week in spring and summer. Unlike markets where part of the charm derives from the surroundings, there's nothing special about a dusty parking lot next to a highway. Instead, this market's appeal comes from its high-quality produce at remarkably reasonable prices. Stand after stand is filled with fruits, vegetables, and herbs that only a few hours earlier were firmly rooted in the earth. You'll also find juices, wine, eggs, honey, jam, cheese, and hummus from local chickpeas.

Eager customers line up at the gate before 6 p.m. The moment it's unlocked, they dash to their favorite sellers. Judging from the crates of produce that some stagger out with, restaurant owners shop here, too. At morning markets the sellers settle in for hours, but here the commerce moves fast. Although the market is open

until 8 p.m., most transactions happen within the first hour. Arrive slightly before opening time for the best selection.

Spring brings asparagus, tender peas, salad greens, and artichokes. Young, violet garlic is milder in flavor than dried garlic. May is prime time for strawberries. The couple who own the farm Mas Tralala (yes, they're singers) explains that cherry season begins in late May with the *Burlats* and continues with other varieties until August.

Farmers bring fuzzy apricots, smooth peaches, and melons in summer. Fresh basil and other herbs perfume the air. Slender *haricots verts* extend over the edges of their containers like dancers' legs perched on the barre. Shiny eggplants, a rainbow of green, red, and yellow peppers, and garlic will be chopped and combined for *ratatouille*. Zucchini blossoms will be stuffed with goat cheese and seasoned with fresh herbs, then their petals twisted to seal them before being lightly fried in olive oil. Most who shop here seem to know what they're doing, but farmers—and other shoppers—are happy to suggest cooking tips if you ask. A farmer with lively blue eyes volunteers that she's 75 years old. When I ask how long she's been farming, she answers with a smile, "I was born into this."

· OTHER WEDNESDAY MARKETS ·

Arles

· MONTHLY FLEA / ANTIQUES MARKET ·

WHEN: *First Wednesday of each month, 8 a.m.–5 p.m.*

WHERE: *Boulevard des Lices*

*I*F YOU ENJOY TREASURE HUNTING and happen to be near Arles on the first Wednesday of the month, you won't want to miss this *brocante*. Roughly 80 sellers are professional dealers. Overall, the quality is good and prices are lower than at L'Isle-sur-la-Sorgue.

All manner of objects turn up: furniture, glassware, jewelry, musical instruments, cameras, silverware, maps, and books. Some are in pristine condition in their original packaging, such as serving pieces in velvet-lined boxes. Many items reflect traditional customs: metal *boules* used in *pétanque,* a game somewhat like horseshoes; Arlessiene skirts, delicate lacework, and velvet ribbons; *santons* (figurines that represent Provençal characters); and tile molds that could be repurposed as trivets.

It's pleasant to walk the length of this market in a leisurely hour under the shade of trees or large umbrellas. Even if one comes away empty-handed, a stroll along Boulevard des Lices with views into the Jardin d'Été might be reward enough.

Beaucaire

❧ · FLEA AND ANTIQUES MARKET · ❧

WHEN: *Wednesday morning, 7 a.m.–noon*

WHERE: *Champ de Foire*

BEAUCAIRE LIES ACROSS the Rhône River from Tarascon. Markets and fairs have been important to Beaucaire since medieval times when King Charles VII declared that Beaucaire would host the annual Foire de Madeleine. The trade fair became famous throughout southern France and endowed the town with impressive architecture, reflecting the wealth of merchants. Upon the arrival of the railroads in the 19th century, the fair diminished in importance and the town's prosperity declined.

Beaucaire's weekly flea market offers a chance to peruse secondhand furniture, linens, pottery, clothing, tins, and other collectibles. The selection runs the gamut, as at any flea market, but shoppers have a chance to spot a treasure that makes the hunt worthwhile. The Foire de Madeleine (also called the Beaucaire Fair) still takes place at the end of July—a tradition since 1217. It's celebrated with a running of the Camargue bulls. Friday evenings during July and August, an arts and crafts market known as Les Beaux Quais de Vendredi sets up along the canal.

Mouriès

· SMALL PROVENÇAL MARKET ·

WHEN: *Wednesday morning*

WHERE: *Village center*

With 80,000 olive trees and an oil-mill cooperative of 400 members, Mouriès claims bragging rights as the olive oil capital of France. Four varieties of olives are grown in the hills along the southern slope of the Alpilles, giving the oils their distinctive flavor. If you do an olive oil tasting—and I recommend it—the subtle flavors might bring to mind fresh-cut grass, raw artichoke, almonds, or cocoa. The local olive oils are classified AOP Vallée des Baux de Provence, which is akin to a gold medal. (For more on olive oils, see p. 121.) Villagers celebrate their bounty with a feast of green olives the third week of September, and another to mark the end of the harvest and the arrival of the new oil in early December. Le Mas de la Tapi, a small shop along the market street, sells quality olive oils and tapenades.

Jean-Benoît and Catherine Hugues, Olive Growers

Olive oil is, like wine, a quintessential expression of Provençal *terroir*. Jean-Benoît Hugues explains the process, "which starts with taking care of the trees." He describes falling in love with their beautiful shapes and complicated needs. "There's no good product without a soul—a history and a connection to the land."

Jean-Benoît and Catherine lived in the United States for 15 years. They returned to France marked by their experiences abroad and a hunger for innovation. They began with 6 hectares in Mouriès, where the olive trees get ideal exposure on the southern slopes of the Alpilles. They gradually acquired orchards in Les Baumettes, Les Baux, and Saint-Rémy and have reached the critical number of hectares to sustain an olive oil business. In addition, they do contract work for other growers at their mill.

They have experimented with the watering system, harvesting methods, and slow-speed grinding—practices

that have helped grow the business. They combine an innovative spirit with an abiding respect for *terroir*. Their oils are extracted cold and made from olives grown exclusively in the Vallée des Baux, distinguished by the AOP (Appellation d'Origine Protégée) status. They produce extra-virgin olive oils, a 100 percent organic version, a fruity oil from black olives, and olive oils with natural accents, such as basil and mint, and thyme and rosemary. Moulin Castelas has won numerous awards. Judging from my own non-scientific taste test, I wager that more will come its way.

Moulin Castelas is at 13520 Les Baux-de-Provence. The shop (where you can taste olive oils and arrange shipping) is open Monday through Friday, 8:30 a.m.–6 p.m.; weekends, 10 a.m.–1 p.m. and 2:30 p.m.–6 p.m. Tel. 04.90.54.50.86. www.castelas.com.

Pernes-les-Fontaines

WHEN: *Wednesday evening, 6–8 p.m., April through October*

WHERE: *Place Frédéric Mistral*

*P*ERNES-LES-FONTAINES was the first village in the Vaucluse to offer a *marché du soir,* or evening market. The experiment succeeded and spawned a dozen others in the *département.* The Vaucluse Chamber of Agriculture regulates the vendors and products at *marché du soir* markets. Sellers must be farmers or producers from the area, and everything must come from their own farms. Locals trust whatever they buy because they know the source.

As the village's name suggests, fountains are the local pride. The discovery of the St. Roch spring meant that villagers no longer had to worry much about drought. They celebrated by building four monumental fountains, and all told there are 40 public fountains throughout the village. A map for the self-guided walking tour Le Circuit des Fontaines is available at the Office de Tourisme on Place Gabriel Moutte.

aGRICULTURES & TERRITOIRES
CHAMBRE D'AGRICULTURE
VAUCLUSE

PerneS
ville d'eau et d'histoire
Les Fontaines

bienvenue à la ferme

Sur cette Place Frédéric Mistral se tient, d'avril à octobre, le Marché du Soir des Producteurs

- Le Marché du Soir des Producteurs est un label délivré par la Chambre d'Agriculture,

- Les vendeurs ne sont que des agriculteurs en activité,

- Les produits sont récoltés du jour et mûris sur la plante,

- Les prix sont ceux de la vente directe,

- Les produits sont exclusivement de saison,

- Les agriculteurs vous parlent de leur métier et de leurs produits,

- Le premier mercredi de chaque mois vous pouvez gagner « Le panier garni du Marché ».

Acheter ici, c'est soutenir les producteurs locaux et c'est faire vivre la Provence !

Thursday

MARKETS

Best

Aix-en-Provence *(traditional Provençal market)*

Avignon *(covered market)*

Nyons *(traditional Provençal market)*

Orange *(traditional Provençal market)*

Roussillon *(traditional Provençal market)*

Velleron *(farmers' market)*, see p. 133

Others

Goult *(traditional Provençal market)*

L'Isle-sur-la-Sorgue *(traditional Provençal market)*

Maussane-les-Alpilles *(traditional Provençal market)*

Ménerbes *(traditional Provençal market)*

Sénas *(farmers' market)*

Villeneuve-lèz-Avignon *(traditional Provençal market)*

Nîmes *(covered market)*, see p. 213

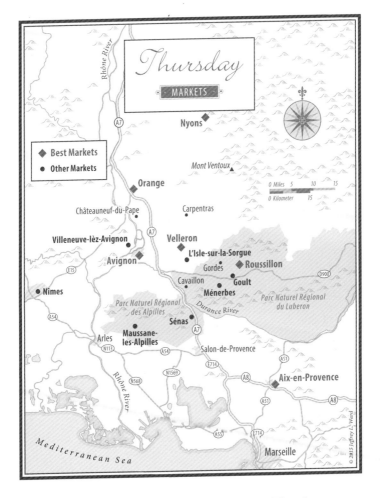

Thursday
◆ MARKETS ◆

◆ **Best Markets**

● **Other Markets**

Rhône River

A7

◆ **Nyons**

Mont Ventoux ▲

0 Miles 5   10   15

0 Kilometer   15

◆ **Orange**

● Châteauneuf-du-Pape

● Carpentras

◆ **Villeneuve-lèz-Avignon**

A7

◆ **Velleron**

◆ **L'Isle-sur-la-Sorgue**

◆ **Avignon**

● Gordes

◆ **Roussillon**

D900

E15

● Cavaillon

◆ **Goult**

Parc Naturel Régional du Luberon

● **Nîmes**

◆ **Ménerbes**

Parc Naturel Régional des Alpilles

Durance River

A54

● **Sénas**

◆ **Maussane-les-Alpilles**

A7

● Arles

N113

A54

Salon-de-Provence

A51

A8

◆ **Aix-en-Provence**

N568

N1569

E714

A8

Rhône River

A51

A55

E714

Mediterranean Sea

Marseille

© 2015 Jeffrey L. Ward

Aix-en-Provence

❧ TRADITIONAL PROVENÇAL MARKET ❧

WHEN: *Daily (although best on Tuesday,*
Thursday, and Saturday mornings)

WHERE: *On Tuesday, Thursday, and Saturday mornings, there*
are food markets at Place des Prêcheurs, Place de la Madeleine,
and Place Richelme; a flower market at Place de l'Hôtel de
Ville; and a flea market at Place de Verdun. On Monday,
Wednesday, Friday, and Sunday mornings, there is a food market
at Place Richelme and a flower market at Place des Prêcheurs.

OFFICE DE TOURISME: *300 Avenue Giuseppe Verdi,*
13100 Aix-en-Provence. Tel: 04.42.16.11.61.
www.aixenprovencetourism.com

ONCE THE CAPITAL OF PROVENCE, Aix-en-Provence is a captivating city with architectural flourishes and gushing fountains. La Fontaine de la Rotonde offers a grand welcome. Water cascades below three statues representing law (facing the city), agriculture (facing Marseille), and art (facing Avignon). The Cours Mirabeau is a wide and handsome street, lined with plane trees and flanked by buildings painted Provençal beiges, pinks, and yellows.

The market in Aix takes place in multiple locations. While the distance between them is not great, the market activity does not always continue on connecting streets, so it's easy to assume that you've seen it all when the best part might be only a block or two farther on. If it's important to you to explore the entire market, go to the Office de Tourisme and request that they mark a route. The office is also an excellent source of information about regional events and activities. The following overview assumes you're visiting the Aix market on a Tuesday, Thursday, or Saturday. Expect some variation on other days.

FOOD MARKET

Make your way to the adjoining squares, Place des Prêcheurs and Place de la Madeleine, with their concentration of fruit, vegetable, and other food stands. A farmer sells apricots and melons as soon as they come into season starting late May or June. Marinated olives, anchovies, and sweet garlic (*ail doux*) in oil and thyme aren't items I buy at home, but here they're an essential part of the local flavor. A honey seller offers a taste of *miel de garrigue* with hints of thyme and rosemary. Nearby, the fury of curry powder and other spices hit the nose, followed by the soothing scent of vanilla from Madagascar.

Tourtons Champsaur—stuffed fried dough—is a specialty from the Hautes-Alpes. An *artisan pâtissier* sells *madeleines* in a choice of almond, vanilla, or plain. His bins empty before the market closes. Les Orchidées offers Asian foods.

More food stands await in Place Richelme in front of the old grain hall. The building's pediment is decorated with depictions of the agricultural bounty. A vendor sells round loaves of bread

made with olive oil and citrus zest. A goat farmer arranges rounds of fresh *chèvre* cheese topped with diced shallots and other toppings. Fishmonger stands overflow with *tellines* (small local clams), oysters, giant prawns, and silvery fishes from the Mediterranean.

FLOWER MARKET

Shoppers cradling bunches of yellow sunflowers or feathered pink peonies are coming from the flower market in Place de l'Hôtel de

Ville, with its buckets of fresh-cut flowers and blooming plants. The backdrop is equally dazzling: Italian-style façades and carved doors, a belfry with an astronomical clock, and a god and goddess dallying on the pediment above the post office.

CLOTHING, TEXTILES, AND FLEA MARKET

Clothing, table linens, and scarves hang from stalls along the broad promenade Cours Mirabeau, and sometimes on Place de Verdun. When the mistral kicks up, they flap like flags on a sailing ship. A small flea market takes place at Place de Verdun, near the Palais de Justice. Silver cutlery, glassware, jewelry, old DVDs, and books can be found there. Judges and lawyers swish by in long black robes as they stride up the steps to court.

OTHER HIGHLIGHTS

Among the stylish shops in Aix are several artisanal purveyors. For cheeses, *fromagerie* André Savelli at 9 Rue des Marseillais and La Fromagerie du Passage at 55 Cours Mirabeau offer good quality. The region's best-known *fromage* is Banon, a goat's-milk cheese wrapped in chestnut leaves. *Brousse du Rove,* a fresh goat cheese, is sold in little plastic cones.

The most famous local specialty is the *calissons d'Aix,* confections made with crushed almonds, honey, and candied orange and melon, and topped with a thin layer of white icing. Legend has it that *calissons* were created for the wedding of King René

The Sweet Life in Provence

While Provence doesn't have unique rights to the biblical phrase, it is the Promised Land for anyone with a sweet tooth. For heavenly treats, try these local specialties.

Calissons d'Aix

A specialty of Aix-en-Provence, these diamond-shaped wafers are topped with a mixture of crushed almonds and candied orange or melon, then crowned with white icing. They taste like fruity marzipan with the crunch of a cookie. Supposedly, they were created for the second wedding of King René in 1454 when the elderly widower wanted to win the heart of his young bride.

- ❦ Béchard, 12 Cours Mirabeau, Aix-en-Provence
- ❦ Puyricard, 7–9 Rue Rifle Rafle, Aix-en-Provence

Fruits Confits

Apt is a center for the manufacture of *confitures* (jams) and *fruits confits*. The latter translates as "candied fruits," but if that brings to mind cloying confections laden with artificial colorings and flavorings, it is misleading. They are the actual fruits, crystallized in syrup, retaining the shape, color, flavor, and a semblance of the texture of the original. The technique originated as a way of preserving the orchards' bounty throughout winter. The process is labor-intensive and delicate. It begins with a careful selection of fruit, then seven rounds of boiling in syrup, cooling, and several months of rest. If the fruits are overcooked, they dissolve into jam. Fruits are either drained of syrup and glazed with a fine layer of sugar, or bottled in syrup, which preserves them for several years. Apricot, melon, strawberry, and clementine are among the popular varieties. *Déclassés egouttés* are fruits that have become misshapen during the process but are more economical for baking. Only a few businesses still make *fruits confits* by the artisanal method. Look for shops that specialize.

- Confiserie Le Coulon—60 Quai de la Liberté, Apt

- Confiserie Marcel Richaud—112 Quai de la Liberté, Apt

- Aptunion—Route 900, Apt (an industrial-scale producer open for tours)

- Lilamand Confiseur—5 Avenue Albert Schweitzer, Saint-Rémy, and 13 Rue de la République, L'Isle-sur-la-Sorgue

- Jouvaud Pâtisserie—40 Rue Evéché, Carpentras

Berlingots

In the 1840s a *pâtissier* from Carpentras came up with a way of using the leftover syrup from *fruits confits:* Blend the syrup with sugar, cook it again at high temperature, pour it onto an oiled marble slab, adorn it with lines of sugar, stretch and fold it, allow it to cool and harden, then cut it into small pieces. Thus the distinctive white-striped *Berlingots* were born. They are handmade by only a few artisanal confectioners.

- ❧ Confiserie Clavel—106 Place Aristide Briand, Carpentras

- ❧ Confiserie du Mont Ventoux—1184 Avenue Dwight Eisenhower, Carpentras

Nougats

This taffylike candy, which comes dark (*nougat noir*) or white (*nougat blanc*), is made with lavender honey, almonds, and fruit. White nougat is softened with egg whites, which makes it chewy. It cooks at a lower temperature but for a longer time than dark nougat. Dark nougat is lightly caramelized and crunchy, with a hint of orange. Both dark and light nougat are among the 13 desserts of the traditional Christmas meal.

- Silvain Paysans Nougatiers—4 Place Neuve, Saint-Didier

- Maison André Boyer Nougatiers—Place de l'Europe, Sault

- Montélimar, a town farther north than the scope of this book, is famous for nougat; Chabert et Guillot is a local artisanal producer.

Honeys

Provençal honeys are especially flavorful and diverse. Local varieties include the subtly fragrant lavender (*lavande*); light and pleasant rosemary (*romarin*); strongly aromatic chestnut (*châtaigne*); a mix of rosemary, thyme, and savory (*garrigue* or *toutes-fleurs*); and dark and pungent oak (*chêne*), which is used in cooked desserts such as fruit compotes. With bee colonies struggling to survive, production is alarmingly low.

Chocolates

While certainly not unique to Provence, high-quality chocolates make any visit that much sweeter. Artisanal *chocolatiers* incorporate local flavors, such as lavender, sea salt, almonds, cherries, and more. Here are some of the best.

- ❧ Puyricard—shops in Aix-en-Provence, Arles, Avignon, and elsewhere

- ❧ La Cour aux Saveurs—2 Rue Louis Lopez, L'Isle-sur-la-Sorgue

- ❧ Joël Durand—3 Boulevard Victor Hugo, Saint-Rémy

- ❧ Peyrerol—7 Cours Henri Fabre, Vaison-la-Romaine

Avignon

◈ · COVERED FOOD MARKET · ◈

WHEN: *Daily except Monday, 8 a.m.–1 p.m.*

WHERE: *Les Halles d'Avignon in Place Pie*

OFFICE DE TOURISME: *41 Cours Jean Jaurès,
84000 Avignon. Tel: 04.32.74.32.74.
www.avignon-tourisme.com*

AVIGNON MAY HAVE REACHED its religious apex 700 years ago when it flourished as the City of the Popes, yet it remains a hub of culture and commerce. The Palace of the Popes towers over red-tiled roofs and bears testament to the period of papal rule. The cherished Pont d'Avignon, familiar from the children's song, juts into the Rhône but no longer crosses to the other side. Stone ramparts that encircle the old city are nearly as daunting to drivers trying to penetrate by car as they were to would-be attackers in the Middle Ages. Notable museums, fine restaurants, and major festivals continue to bring this city distinction and make it throb with activity.

Another attraction and tradition is shopping at the covered food market, Les Halles d'Avignon. After one wends through narrow cobblestone streets past stone buildings sagging with age, the market's façade—a green wall of plants—appears like a mad botany

Thursday ❀ 161

experiment gone very right. Tulips and hyacinths in buckets at the market's entry look as if they might have tumbled from it.

Inside Les Halles, about 40 stalls are stocked with high-quality regional foods. Cheeses, sweets, wines, olive oils, and fresh produce take center stage. Au Panier displays *fruits, confits,* and *calissons d'Aix,* traditional Provençal sweets (see p. 156). At Maison Feste dry-cured sausages hang like a *rideau de buis,* a curtain of wooden or ceramic beads. This *charcuterie* also sells smoked salmon, eel, and *poutargue* (mullet eggs).

Florian Judicaël, the owner of Serge Olives, has been selling olives and tapenades in Les Halles for 20 years. He took over the business from his great-uncle, who owned it the previous 38 years. That's typical of these sellers. Most are family businesses that have been handed down through generations.

La Maison du Fromage boasts over 250 kinds of cheese from Provence and beyond. The number climbs during the holidays with seasonal varieties. Madame Francoz explains that the name Roquefort, like Champagne, is tightly regulated and limited to a specific geographical region and set of standards. Made from raw sheep's milk in Rocquefort-sur-Souizon, Rocquefort was the first cheese to become AOC (Appellation d'Origine Contrôlée) certified in 1925, setting it apart from other varieties of blue cheese. She also sells eggs and *le beurre Bordier,* a butter favored by chefs that comes in variations such as *espelette* (mild pepper), *sel fumé* (smoky salt), and *yuzu* (citrus).

Fishmonger La Marée Provençale displays the gleaming fresh catch. Café Cabane d'Oléron serves platters of shellfish. Oysters are the specialty at Le Jardin des Coquillages. You can try various sizes and types without doing any of the nasty shucking yourself. Several eateries provide casual seating and serve wine.

The market is busy on weekends. Chefs and others with discerning taste make a ritual of shopping at this market. (See p. 28.) Sellers are usually friendly and might mug for the camera. A butcher holds up a rabbit, its fur still shiny, so tourists can snap photos.

If you're not filled to brimming by the time you leave Les Halles, you can find refreshment across from the market along Place Pie (a reference to Pope Pius), sometimes called Pie Square. Cafés offer terrace seating with a good vantage point on the market as shoppers stream in and out. Place de l'Horloge is another popular gathering spot in the heart of Avignon with neoclassical buildings and an antique carousel. Street performers entertain the crowds, which swell in July when Avignon hosts a major theater festival (the Festival d'Avignon) and an "Off" fringe festival of experimental works.

Avignon also hosts a small flea market in Place Pie on Tuesday and Thursday mornings, and in Place des Carmes on Sunday. On Friday, a flower market blossoms in Place des Carmes.

Chef Julien Charvet

The first time I see Chef Charvet, he is leading a class at Les Halles d'Avignon for a group of British tourists. One woman insists she is a novice and demonstrates it by having difficulty tying on her apron. With humor and patience, he assists her and then slides back into the intricacies of filleting fish. During another visit, I watch him teach children how to make crêpes for Candlemas. He shows them how to measure and weigh ingredients, peel and dice vegetables without hurting themselves, and break eggs on a flat surface rather than on a bowl's edge.

Whether he's teaching adults or children, his classes always include an excursion through the covered market to find ingredients. He picks up a mango and gently squeezes it. "If it gives slightly, it's ripe." He is uncompromising about eating fruits and vegetables only when they are in season. "I wouldn't think of eating strawberries in February." He looks aghast as he considers it. "They have no flavor!"

I take one of his classes and learn to prepare fish soup with Marseillaise *rouille* sauce, sole *meunière* with steamed potatoes, and the classic "kings' cake," or *galette des rois* (also called *Pithivier* for the town where they are said to have originated) made with layers of puff pastry and almond cream filling. Inspecting our progress, he erupts with *"C'est parfait!"* which keeps up our strength as we continue whisking. Regardless of age or experience, his students develop skills and confidence while having fun—and a good meal afterward.

Charvet learned how to cook at the side of his father, who was chef at a restaurant in Paris. Now his own children accompany him in the kitchen, where he is passing the skills to the next generation.

For information about "Concept Chef" classes, go to www.conceptchef.com.

Nyons

WHEN: *Thursday morning*

WHERE: *Town center*

OFFICE DE TOURISME: *Place de la Libération,
26111 Nyons. Tel: 04.75.26.10.35. www.paysdenyons.com*

THANKS TO A MICROCLIMATE that's full of sunshine but largely shielded from wind, the landscape around Nyons shimmers with silver-green leaves of olive trees. The highly regarded Nyons olives, called *Tanche,* are jet black, lightly wrinkled, slightly salty, and popular eating olives. The olive oil is mild and fruity with a hint of hazelnut. Nicknamed the *perle noire,* or black pearl of Provence, Nyons olives received an AOC designation in 1994.

Another attraction is the large market, which has been held on Thursday morning since the Middle Ages. When locals speak highly of a market, as they do about Nyons, it's often expressed as "you can find everything." From soaps to spices, from fruits to flowers, from olives to oils, from cheese to chintz—it's all here.

Part of what makes the Nyons market one of the best in northern Provence is that many local producers participate. Moulin Ramade sells olives, oils, and tapenades. Rocher Florin brings *chèvre.* Régis and Corinne Pacalon grow their fruits and vegetables in Piégon. La Condamine, from Bésignan, sells fruits, juices, and honey. Tender and tasty lamb from Sisteron can be found at the butcher Usclat. Fishmongers, florists, and souvenir sellers round out the offerings. Dos Amigos entertains shoppers with flamenco music, while the Bad Boys trio plays toe-tapping jazz.

A cooperative of about 1,100 growers operates Vignolis, a shop with olive oils, wines, and other local products at 6 Avenue Venterol. For historical interest, La Scourtinerie (36 Rue de la Maladrerie) is the last workshop to produce *scourtins*. These coconut-fiber mats look like large place mats and were used in traditional olive pressing to filter the oil.

Nyons also hosts a smaller market on Sunday morning, mid-May to mid-September, which features local crafts and produce.

Orange

WHEN: *Thursday morning*

WHERE: *Town center*

OFFICE DE TOURISME: *5 Cours Aristide Briand,*
84100 Orange. Tel: 04.90.34.70.88.
www.otorange.fr

ROMAN EMPERORS knew better than to keep well-trained soldiers close to home after they had completed their service. Thus colonies were established in Orange, Vaison-la-Romaine, and elsewhere in Provence as communities for retired military personnel—at a safe distance from Rome. In roughly 35 BC, builders constructed Orange with iconic elements of Roman architecture. Two remain in fine form to this day: the Roman Theatre, made of golden stone and with nearly perfect acoustics (an opera festival and other performances are held in this open-air venue in the summer), and the Triumphal Arch, located on the ancient Via Agrippa that connected Lyon to Arles. UNESCO has designated both structures as World Heritage sites.

The town's rich history extends to the market as well, which has been a Thursday tradition since 1428. In the fall, *pleurottes, cêpes,* and other mushrooms abound, along with *potimarron* (pumpkin) and other squashes. In summer, crates are heaped with melons, tomatoes, cherries, and apricots. The fish at Sérignan du Comtat are predominantly from local waters. Aux Arômes de Provences sells spices that will add flavor to any recipe. And no Provençal market would be complete without goat cheese, such as those sold at Valière. Honey varieties include lavender, rosemary, and chestnut, depending on the season.

Supplementing the options at market, several shops feature regional products. Le Comptoir des Gourmets (1 Rue Notre Dame) sells *croquant soufflé aux noisettes,* crunchy hazelnut biscuits. Les Fromages de Pache (18 Rue de la République) offers *Banon* goat cheese among other choices. Pâtisserie Carpentier (9 Rue Pourtoules) makes a cookie topped with crystallized orange peel. Ferme des Quatre Saisons (85 Avenue de Lattre de Tassigny) is a cooperative that sells eggs, fruit juices, nuts, and grains. Heading out of Orange toward Jonquières, you can find locally cultivated saffron at Les Safranières d'Arausio on Chemin de Ramas.

Orange is centrally located in the Côtes du Rhône wine region, home to the well-known vineyards of Chateauneuf-du-Pâpe, Gigondas, and Vacqueyras. The Côté Rhône wine shop (19 Place Clemenceau) has a selection of Rhône valley wines. In the surrounding countryside, rows of grapevines and olive trees occasionally open up to views across the plains to Mont Ventoux and the chiseled Dentelles de Montmirail.

For a view of the Roman Theatre from a distance (and no entry fee), hike to the top of the bluff in the Parc de la Colline Saint-Eutrope. The grassy park makes a good spot for digging into those bundles of market purchases.

Roussillon

WHEN: *Thursday morning*

WHERE: *Village center*

OFFICE DE TOURISME: *Place de la Poste,*
84220 Roussillon. Tel: 04.90.05.60.25

*I*N A REGION thick with golden-gray limestone, the sudden appearance of red cliffs and orange soil makes a startling sight. This is the quirky geology of Roussillon, which sits atop ochre deposits. The ochre veins were mined for their pigments until 1930, when the last quarry closed. The colorful village gets crowded with tourists, but it's definitely worth a visit.

On market days the sellers set up their stands in front of buildings painted orange, yellow, and pink. Silky olive oil soaps come in a similar rainbow, each with its own sweet fragrance. Lavender sachets, scarves, children's clothing, herbs, and spices are easy to tuck into a suitcase. Some crafts are original creations, such as the glass jewelry made by Sylvain Ange. A woman sews table coverings from fabric that she buys near Strasbourg.

Strawberries from Carpentras and nectarines in orange-red hues evoke the ochre cliffs. Signs indicate where each item was grown. Asparagus are gathered in bunches so tight they look like a family huddling against the mistral. A woman sells honey; her husband is the *apiculteur.* There are homemade jams, tapenades, cheeses, and cookies flavored with orange blossom. Or try pizza topped with olives, a Provençal standby.

It doesn't take long to explore the market. Afterward, you can walk the Ochre Trail (Sentier des Ocres), a hiking path beside a

former quarry. There are long and short options, but you don't need to go far to get a view of the yellows, oranges, and reds that streak the hills. It's worth a scramble as long as you don't mind a long-lasting souvenir: clothing and shoes sprinkled with red dust. It's possible to buy a combination ticket for entrance to both the Ochre Trail and the Ochre Conservatory, which you can visit after leaving Roussillon on the road to Apt. Located in the former Mathieu ochre factory, this educational center explains how ochre was extracted and why the demand for pigments rose in the late 18th century because of the textile industry.

Shops, galleries, and cafés line the cobblestoned streets of Roussillon. Au Goût du Jour on Rue Richard Casteau sells regional specialties, including candied fruits (*fruits confits*), olive oils, and *calissons d'Aix*. The proprietor can help you choose a local wine. Continue up Rue d'Église for views that stretch across the Luberon to the Monts de Vaucluse. Architectural details and pastel shutters will delight the attentive eye. Late afternoons are especially pleasant for relaxing at an outdoor table and observing the village. You'll be following in the footsteps of American sociologist Laurence Wylie, whose study of Roussillon in the 1950s developed into *A Village in the Vaucluse* and became a classic about secluded rural life. (He disguised Roussillon with the fictitious name Peyrane.)

Roussillon is now one of the most highly visited places in the Luberon. As you depart, the red cliffs recede and then disappear, but their image is likely engraved in your memory forever.

Catherine Pisani, Basil Farmer

While mixing clays with plant extracts to create health and beauty products, Catherine Pisani discovered the heady perfume given off by basil. It inspired her to shift her farm to primarily basil cultivation. She sows 60 varieties. In any given year, about half are successful. They range from the basic green Genoa basil to esoteric ones that are used in Ayurvedic medicine. She starts the seeds in her greenhouse and then transplants them to the field in front of her beautiful stone home.

Basil season runs from mid-July until October. The leaves cannot be easily preserved, but she takes them to Arôma Plantes in Sault, where they are distilled to create oils and floral essences. She has begun selling *Berlingot* candies that a local confectioner produces specially for her, flavoring them with basil varieties that she provides: cinnamon, lemon, anise, and classic green.

Catherine sells her plants and products at the Sunday market in Coustellet, the Tuesday farmers' market in Apt, and the Thursday market in Saignon.

La Ferme aux Basilics is at La Décane, 84220 Roussillon. Look for the sign along the D900 between Coustellet and Apt, near the Pont Julien. www.lafermeauxbasilics.com.

· SMALL PROVENÇAL MARKET ·

WHEN: *Thursday morning from April to October*

WHERE: *Village center*

PERCHED ON A HILL with views toward the Luberon, Mont Ventoux, and the Monts de Vaucluse, Goult is within easy distance of more frequently visited hilltop villages such as Gordes and Lacoste. Yet being set back from the main thoroughfare helps this village preserve its quiet charm.

Goult is a rare example of a Provençal village that changed its market day. It used to be held on Monday, but in 2013 it shifted to Thursday. Only a few vendors show up, yet there's a large amount of socializing and civic pride. Across the street, Café de la Poste buzzes with customers. For dinner, the restaurant La Bartavelle has a good reputation.

A narrow road leads up to the oldest part of the village, where a 12th-century castle, old windmill, and vaulted passages seem to have grown out of the local golden stone. Goult hosts a honey festival the third Sunday in July. But no matter when you visit, you will likely find it a sweet spot.

L'Isle-sur-la-Sorgue

· SMALL PROVENÇAL MARKET ·

WHEN: *Thursday morning*

WHERE: *Town center*

THE MAIN MARKET DAY in L'Isle-sur-la-Sorgue is Sunday, when the entire town springs to life with a food market plus Provence's largest weekly antiques and flea market (see p. 19). The much smaller Thursday market includes none of the roving *brocante* dealers; even the permanent antiques shops and galleries are closed. The focus, instead, is on regional foods: breads, olives, honey, cheese, fish, and roasted meats. Market stands form a semi-circle around the church Nôtre-Dame-des-Anges, with a few more in Place Rose Goudard.

Although the Thursday market is small potatoes compared to Sunday's extravaganza, it offers a chance to explore the town without the crowds. You'll have a better chance of getting close-up shots of the moss-covered waterwheels and emerald canals—and of getting a table at one of the fine restaurants or on the terrace of Café de France.

Maussane-les-Alpilles

◆ SMALL PROVENÇAL MARKET ◆

WHEN: *Thursday morning*

WHERE: *Village center*

Tucked into the heart of Les Baux valley and surrounded by olive orchards, pine forests, and rocky outcroppings, Maussane is one of the prettiest villages in the Alpilles. Two women sip espressos at a café while their children pedal scooters around a fountain that celebrates the four seasons. Maussane's market is easy to navigate, and the quality is good. *Légumes Direct Producteur* indicates that the seller is a farmer and the produce has come directly from his fields. The line of customers at the fishmonger's stall stays the same length all morning, and fresh fish move out just as fast as new shoppers swim in. A woman sells attractive handcrafted pottery in yellows and greens that evoke the local landscape. Smooth olive wood with swirls of brown in the grain has been fashioned into heart-shaped plates and mortars and pestles.

This is one of the top areas in France for olive oil production. Don't leave without visiting an olive oil mill where the local ambrosia is created (see p. 121).

Ménerbes

WHEN: *Thursday morning, April to October*

WHERE: *Village center*

DESIGNATED one of the Most Beautiful Villages of France (a distinction that's shared with Ansouis, Gordes, Lourmarin, Roussillon, and Venasque), Ménerbes soared in popularity when British author Peter Mayle settled here and featured it as the setting for *A Year in Provence*. His fans swarmed the village for years afterward. But Mayle moved, and Ménerbe's true nature as a quiet outpost has returned.

The village stretches along the crest of a cliff. Nostradamus nicknamed it *vaisseau phantome,* or ghostly vessel. Sure enough, it resembles a ship floating in a sea of vines and cherry orchards. You'll find cheeses, fruits and vegetables, rotisserie chicken, and a few souvenirs at the market. Ménerbes also hosts a truffle market on the last Sunday of December.

Don't despair if you don't happen to be in Ménerbes on its one truffle market day; you're still in luck. At the summit of the village in a 17th-century mansion, next to the clock tower, is Maison de la Truffe et du Vin, with a truffle menu and excellent wine selection. Views from the terrace tables are stunning. An unusual attraction about 2 km north of Ménerbes is a corkscrew museum, La Musée du Tire-Bouchon, at Domaine de la Citadelle.

Sénas

WHEN: *From June to September, every morning except Sunday and public holidays; from October to May, Monday, Wednesday, Friday, and Saturday mornings*

WHERE: *Place Auguste Jaubert*

*I*T'S HARDLY MORE than a roadside stop, but quality produce and friendly farmers make this market worth a brief visit if you happen to be in the area. Purple radishes, red-skinned potatoes, striped melons, and flowering plants animate this *marché paysan*. You can come away with not only some of the region's freshest seasonal produce but also a few tips on how best to cook and store them. Every Thursday morning, Sénas hosts a small traditional Provençal market with the typical array of foods, fabrics, and clothing, but it's the authentic farmers' market that makes this small village in the Alpilles worth its mention.

Villeneuve-lèz-Avignon

WHEN: *Thursday morning*

WHERE: *Place Charles David*

VILLENEUVE-LÈZ-AVIGNON is better known for its Saturday flea and antiques market (p. 250), but insiders know that the Thursday food market can also reward visitors with good finds. Sunflowers with faces big as dinner plates, *Tomme* cheeses, seasonal fruits and vegetables, and Mediterranean fish are typical offerings. Villeneuve-lèz-Avignon lies at the crossroads of Provence and Languedoc, and its market attracts vendors selling specialties from both regions.

Friday

• MARKETS •

Best

Bonnieux *(traditional Provençal market)*

Carpentras *(traditional Provençal market)*

Eygalières *(traditional Provençal market)*

Lourmarin *(traditional Provençal market)*

Nîmes *(covered market)*

Avignon *(covered market)*, see p. 161

Velleron *(farmers' market)*, see p. 133

Fontvieille *(traditional Provençal market)*, see p. 57

Others

Lambesc *(traditional Provençal market)*

Pertuis *(traditional Provençal market)*

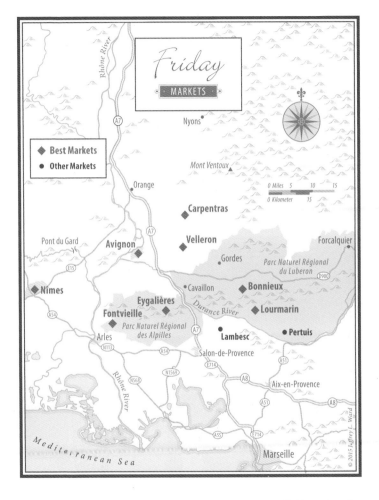

Bonnieux

WHEN: *Friday morning*

WHERE: *Village center*

OFFICE DE TOURISME: *7 Place Carnot, 84480 Bonnieux.*
Tel: 04.90.75.91.90. www.tourisme-en-luberon.com

THE MEDIEVAL VILLAGE of Bonnieux clings to a narrow edge of the Luberon. Old buildings and ancient stone walls look dangerously unstable, yet they've withstood their precarious perch for centuries. The drive to Bonnieux consists of twisty roads that climb the mountain, with views over the valley toward Lacoste, Gordes, Roussillon, and, in the distance, Mont Ventoux. If you approach from the north, you are likely to pass Pont Julien, an arched stone bridge across the Calavon River that the Romans built around 3 BC. The bridge was in use until 2005, when vehicular crossings were permanently banned. Coming from the south, the road narrows outside Lourmarin and cuts a winding path between the Petit and Grand Luberon past dense pine forests and limestone crevasses—a scenic route that includes a few white-knuckle turns.

The picturesque setting makes this market special. It draws a mix of locals who come to stock up on meat, fish, vegetables, and other essentials, and travelers who want to experience a village market with local foods and crafts. The market starts in the lower section of the village in front of the "new" church, built in 1870, with craft and souvenir vendors. The market continues up a sloped street and spreads out to fill the level (finally!) square. Bicyclists huff and puff as they pedal the last leg of a steep climb. Parents push baby carriages up the hill. Others pull shopping carts along the bumpy pavement with wheels squeaking as they slowly advance. Friends pause as much to catch their breath as to catch up on each other's news.

The upper section, on Place Gambetta, is where you'll find most of the food and flower stalls. Local *producteurs* bring honeys, fruit jams, and crusty loaves of bread. Rounds of fresh goat cheese are topped with black peppercorns, chopped scallions, or shiny red pepper flakes. Lavender soaps and lotions might be wrapped with a blue sprig. Herbs and spices come in many varieties, including pink salts, golden turmeric, and deep green *herbes de Provence,* a mixture of dried savory, rosemary, thyme, and sometimes a few pinches of lavender from the Provençal hillsides.

Garlic bulbs are sold individually or in braided tresses. Rolland Tranchimand, a local farmer, has crates of miniature eggplants and zucchinis, plus bottles of pickled "minis." He also brings zucchini flowers that look like giant tulips veined green and yellow. Stuff them with goat cheese and lightly fry for a finger-licking start to a meal. Spring and summer bring a succession of local strawberries, cherries, apricots, melons, grapes, and figs.

Olive-wood utensils, table linens, and baskets make attractive souvenirs. The quality is good, and the prices are reasonable. Local artists sell pottery and oil paintings. One woman's ceramic dishes, glazed with swirling yellows and greens, are so pretty that I convince myself I need another butter plate.

Cafés and restaurants around the square make use of their terraces under the shade of chestnut trees. Glacier Le Tinel serves homemade ice cream. Fort-de-Buoux, a few kilometers east of Bonnieux, or the cool and welcoming Forêt de Cèdres, a few kilometers south toward Lourmarin, are excellent picnic spots.

The bread-baking museum in Bonnieux sounds intriguing, but the displays are uninspired. Another specialty museum in Ménerbes, at Domaine de la Citadelle, is a collection of over a thousand corkscrews that range from utilitarian to extravagant. Or simply uncork a beverage in Bonnieux and soak up the sights and sounds. When the bells chime, it feels as if the scene has sprung out of a jewelry box. Birds perch on a stone wall, waiting for vagrant crumbs, and then take tremulous flight over the valley.

Carpentras

WHEN: *Friday morning*

WHERE: *Town center and Allée des Platanes (and a truffle market from mid-November to March at Hôtel-Dieu)*

OFFICE DE TOURISME: *97 Place du 25 Août 1944, 84200 Carpentras. Tel: 04.90.63.00.78. www.carpentras-ventoux.com*

CARPENTRAS PROSPERED under the Romans, who built upon what their Gallic predecessors had begun. Once known as Carpentoracte, or "city of chariots," because so many traveled here for commerce, prosperous Carpentras was designated the capital of the Comtat Venaissin, the powerful pontifical state that remained independent of the kingdom of France until 1791. The Carpentras market began in 1151, making it the oldest in Provence.

The market fills the heart-shaped center of Carpentras and, like oxygenated blood being pumped into arteries, spills into side streets and flows as far as the Allée des Platanes on the eastern edge of town. Vendors sell fruits and vegetables, cheese, honey, spices and herbs, olives, meat, and fish. Clothing, tablecloths, flowers, and souvenirs lend variety to the mix. Quality and price vary from stall to stall. Arab vendors cluster along Rue Cottier.

On Fridays during black truffle season, "black diamonds" from

Fraise de Carpentr

CARPENTRAS COMTAT VENAISSIN

the nearby countryside and the slopes of Mont Ventoux add another dimension to the market. The truffle market begins at 9 a.m. by the Hôtel-Dieu (see p. 269).

Carpentras has many agricultural riches, but it's best known for strawberries, starting in mid-April and continuing through June. During one spring visit, I have the happy coincidence of meeting the head pastry chef of Fauchon from Paris. A French television

crew films him deftly slicing *fraises de Carpentras* obtained at Fruits Primeurs, a produce shop on Rue des Halles.

Carpentras is also famous for *Berlingots*. These hard candies were supposedly created in the 14th century when Pope Clement V was living in Carpentras. Traditional *Berlingots* were red colored and mint flavored, although now they are available in a range of colors and flavors. *Berlingots de Carpentras* are sold in many shops, but the best are made by artisanal methods (see p. 158).

Several notable shops dot the warren of streets. The highly regarded La Fromagerie du Comtat at 23 Place Maurice Charretier has been in the Vigier family since 1982. The cheese selection changes with the seasons.

Pâtisserie Jouvaud at 40 Rue de l'Evêché will delight anyone with a sweet tooth. *Rocailles* (mountains of meringue in vanilla, chocolate, or coffee) and other confections are made on the premises. A few doors down at 9 Rue de l'Evêché, the J. E. Turquin art gallery sells paintings and posters that evoke market scenes and local landscapes. Passage Boyer is positioned between what once had been the fish market and the herb and potato market. The glass-covered passageway borrows its style from the 19th-century *passages couvertes* in Paris.

The Carpentras synagogue, in Place Maurice Charretier, is the oldest in existence in France. A sizable Jewish community lived in Carpentras in the 12th and 13th centuries. There are no regular tours, but Madame Levy kindly opened the doors and led me into the sanctuary. It's a jewel box of green pastel walls, brass candelabras, and wood columns painted in trompe l'oeil style.

If you're hungry, Chez Serge at 90 Rue Cottier offers a decent meal at reasonable prices, featuring black truffles in winter and white truffles in summer. The owner occasionally offers cooking classes that begin with a market tour.

Carpentras holds a weekly flea market on Sunday (see p. 37) and a Tuesday evening farmers' market from April to September.

Eygalières

WHEN: *Friday morning*

WHERE: *Village center*

ONE OF THE LOVELIEST VILLAGES in the Alpilles, Eygalières exudes a sense of calm. A clock tower at the peak of the hill marks the hour like a stern taskmaster, and yet life around it abides by its own timetable: Olives slowly ripen in the groves, and vines lazily creep along stone walls. Wild herbs release their fragrances while villagers sleep. It's no wonder that celebrities escape to second homes in this enclave with its quiet charm, handsome setting, and good restaurants.

On market morning, villagers throw open their periwinkle and pewter-colored wooden shutters with more than usual anticipation of the day. Vendors set up stands along Rue de la République with fruits and vegetables, cheese, meats, olives, honey, nougat, and olive oils. Thin slices of *baguette* spread with *pistou rouge* are handed out at Sous le Soleil. Shoppers line up for succulent roasted chickens at Poulet Rôti, while others head to the paella seller or to the Asian stand where scents of lemongrass and onion waft from freshly prepared foods.

Striped and solid colored espadrilles, market baskets, linens, and pottery come in vivid hues. Clothing, soaps, jewelry, and handbags add to the pageantry. I buy a plum-colored crocheted

vest, called a *cache-coeur*; the vendor sells them in about ten colors. The *draps de hamman* aren't too bulky for the suitcase. Large ones serve as an attractive cover for chairs and tables; small ones make absorbent bath towels. Local artisans sell jewelry and drawings. Vintage prints of Provence are organized by village name. After thumbing through the entire collection, I select a tinted photograph from 1905 that depicts shoppers in their finery strolling along Boulevard des Lices in Arles.

The quality at this market is high, and the mood couldn't be more pleasant. Linger over a refreshing drink where you can sit outside and watch the market activity or the bicyclists who pedal past. Both Café de la Place and Le Progrès make good perches. Sous Les Micocouliers is one of several restaurants that do a fine job of presenting local, seasonal ingredients in creative ways.

An accordion player with a black bowler hat serenades the shoppers and sellers. I take a photo, and he nods to another hat, upside down on the ground in front of him. I toss in a few coins—a small price to pay for live background music. No matter how long you stay, it will be hard to pull away from this charming village with its exceptional market.

Noëlie Combel,
Fruit and Vegetable Farmer

A farm of only 3 hectares, La Grange di Blound produces fruits and vegetables of exceptional quality. *Clery* strawberries and *Burlats,* the earliest cherries of the season, are among the best I tasted, as are their homemade fruit nectars and marmalades. Noëlie, her father, Lucien, and I walk the fields together one spring morning, gently pushing back leaves to admire the strawberries reddening and the zucchinis lengthening before our eyes.

Noëlie is the fourth generation of Combels to tend this land. With her new baby, the fifth generation will soon be in training. Noëlie's parents sold produce at markets, but she prefers selling directly at the farm. "It's more personally satisfying," she says, and her customers appreciate eating food whose origins they can see with their own eyes. The variety of crops keeps them coming back throughout the growing season, from spring harvests of strawberries and *petit pois* through fall's squashes and pumpkins. In between, it's cherries, melons, apricots, figs, peaches, apples, beans, salad greens, cucumbers, tomatoes, peppers, eggplant, and zucchini. Customers are welcome to augment their purchases with a handful of aromatic herbs.

Noëlie and Lucien wipe their brows when describing the long hours of farmwork. Then Lucien shifts his glance toward Mont Ventoux and adds, "But with this scenery, every day is like a holiday."

La Grange di Blound is at 259 Chemin du Mauvais Pas, 84330 Modène. The farm stand is open April to October, 10 a.m.–noon and 4 p.m.–7 p.m., daily except Saturday afternoon and Sunday.

Lourmarin

❧ TRADITIONAL PROVENÇAL MARKET ❧

WHEN: *Friday morning*

WHERE: *Village center*

OFFICE DE TOURISME: *Place Henri Barthélémy,
84160 Lourmarin. Tel: 04.90.68.10.77. www.lourmarin.com*

THE PETIT LUBERON and the Grand Luberon—mountains that form the mighty Luberon range—rise steeply to the north of Lourmarin. The village lies at the entrance to a pass that's chiseled between them. At night, moonlight traces the mountains' black profile. In daylight, when the sun clears the peaks and casts an amber glow across the village, old stone buildings turn golden. It's fitting that the village is designated one of the Most Beautiful Villages of France—an honor that's shared by only six other villages in the Vaucluse.

The beauty of Lourmarin contributes to the popularity of its market. It is busiest from Easter through mid-October, when roughly 200 vendors serve a mix of locals and tourists. Plane trees lead toward the village center, where cobbled lanes are lined with centuries-old houses, boutiques, art galleries, restaurants, and cafés. Bells peal from two different towers, although neither lands exactly on the hour. An impressive castle and a pasture form an idyllic backdrop. Squeals of children playing soccer and a braying donkey add to the bucolic feel. Lourmarin is also blessed with generous parking, some under the low-hanging branches of well-endowed fig and cherry trees.

Like other village markets in Provence, this one follows the crooked contours of the streets. Place Barthélémy, the plaza near the Office de Tourisme, is a main hub. But the market spills into several squares and spreads along winding streets. Vendors put effort into the presentation of their wares. Baskets are lined with red and yellow Provençal cloths before being filled with *saucissons*.

Golden loaves of *fougasse* are stacked in orderly patterns. Fishmongers lay out the fresh catch on white beds of ice. Fronds of fresh dill and sprigs of wild thyme add flourishes to other displays.

Goat cheeses, a Provençal specialty, never disappoint with their earthy flavor. Even if you think that you don't like the taste of goat cheese, give the local varieties a chance. They're sometimes sprinkled with ash or wrapped in chestnut leaves. Sweet and juicy Carpentras strawberries are sold by the *barquette,* and eggplants gleam so brightly they look as if they've been hand-polished.

Customers form a line at a bread vendor's table where long loaves have been scored on the diagonal to make crusty ridges. Shorter, denser loaves are studded with raisins, figs, and apricots. Others are stuffed with cheese and tomatoes. A seller at Nos Saveurs Provençales smears tomato and onion *confit* atop slices of *baguette* as samples. *Pistou de basilic* (basil with olive oil and garlic) is a key ingredient in traditional Provençal soup. Fig jam will add a sweet note to *foie gras.* Les Saveurs du Sud also sells spreads and sauces that feature local flavors: Sun-dried tomato and olive, or artichoke and garlic, exclaims "Provence" with every bite.

Saucissons come in about 20 varieties. In addition to pork, there's wild boar, bull, and duck—sometimes with a dusting of herbs. An oyster seller demonstrates how to pry open the shells. He lets me practice on one. I buy a dozen and hope I'll be able to replicate his technique.

An *apiculteur* takes his bee boxes to different locations to create specific flavors of honey, such as *miel de sapin* (pine) and *miel de lavendre.* Nougat candies make good use of the local honey and

nuts. *Calissons* are a specialty of Aix-en-Provence. If your itinerary doesn't extend as far as Aix, try them here.

Local crafts include paintings, photographs, and jewelry. Other vendors sell items that they didn't make themselves but still evoke the colors and character of Provence: ceramic grinders filled with *herbes de Provence,* toys that chirp like cicadas, and small dishes for scraping garlic. Market baskets, scarves, pottery, and table linens always delight with their vibrant colors. Cotton *boutis* (traditional Provençal bed covers) come in quieter tones. For gifts, *savons de Marseille,* soaps made with olive oil or lavender, are easy to transport.

Meander in the maze of streets to discover the village's quaint shops. Twisting paths might be disorienting at first, but you will eventually return to a familiar spot. La Maison d'Ingrid, a gourmet *épicerie* on Rue du Temple, sells regional specialties. Le Moulin Dauphin specializes in olive oils that were pressed in Cucuron. The wine cooperative Louérion sells Luberon wines. Over 100 growers from Lourmarin, Cadenet, Lauris, and Curcuron participate in this cooperative—hence the name that presumes to combine them.

The Château de Lourmarin hosts musical performances in summer. For a schedule of performances, visit www.chateau-de-lourmarin.com, and buy tickets in advance if possible.

Les Caves du Château wine bar is tucked near the stairs leading to the gardens. Or walk to the cemetery where Albert Camus is buried. The voices of commerce and social life will begin to fade, replaced by gurgling fountains and melodious birdsong.

Chef Reine Sammut

Reine Sammut's nickname—the Queen of Provençal Cooking—is a play on her name (*reine* means "queen") and a title she has earned during her forty-year reign in the kitchen, turning out one majestic meal after another. She and daughter Nadia operate two restaurants at the country inn Auberge La Fenière. One serves gastronomic fare that's broadly Mediterranean, and the other offers informal dining, taking a creative approach to accommodating diners with gluten or lactose allergies or other dietary restrictions. Golden hues that echo the farmhouse stone give the bistro its relaxed, even mood, while the dining room at Auberge makes a formal first impression with creased napkins and white tablecloths. But there's an electrifying streak: Cobalt blue, burnt orange, and flame red enliven the furnishings. It's as if the mistral roared through, upending an artist's palette and splashing color across the room.

A combination of seriousness and play seems to define Reine's style. She wears a white chef's jacket, blue jeans, red-rimmed glasses, and ochre sneakers. Short auburn hair frames an impish twinkle in her eyes. A tall sculpture of cutlery painted brash blue stands at the entrance.

Everything suggests serious ambition combined with irrepressible lightheartedness.

Chef Sammut credits her mother-in-law with teaching her how to cook. Her husband Guy is a musician, but years ago his father insisted that he have another way to make money if he was going to start a family. His parents helped the couple open a restaurant. Reine's mother-in-law taught her family recipes, which reflected their Sicilian roots. Reine thrived in the apprenticeship and proved herself an uncommonly skilled chef.

I ask why there aren't more female chefs in Provence. "It's very difficult to work in a kitchen and have a family life. I like to cook, but I don't have much time with my family." As if on cue, two young granddaughters race toward Reine's lap.

What advice does she have for those shopping the markets in Provence? A serious expression crosses her face. "It's important to find the local producers. For food, go to the farmers' markets." With that, she picks up one of her granddaughters and takes her outside to play.

Auberge La Fenière is on D943 (between Lourmarin and Cadenet), 84160 Cadenet. Tel: 04.90.68.11.79. www.reine sammut.com

Nîmes

· COVERED FOOD MARKET ·

WHEN: *Daily, 7 a.m.–1 p.m. (many stalls are closed on Monday)*

WHERE: *Les Halles de Nîmes at 5 Rue des Halles*

OFFICE DE TOURISME: *6 Rue Auguste, 30020
Nîmes. Tel: 04.66.58.38.00. www.ot-nimes.fr*

Nîmes LIES WEST of Avignon and Arles on the opposite side of the Rhône. Situated on the Via Domitia that links Rome to Spain, Nîmes thrived as a center of commerce and culture. Roman remains continue to shape the city's identity. A 20,000-seat amphitheatre is considered one of the best preserved of the Roman world, and the Maison Carrée temple rivals the Pantheon as one of the most intact specimens of the Roman Empire. The Pont du Gard, an aqueduct that brought water from Uzès to Nîmes, is a marvel of Roman engineering only 19 km away. After the period of Roman rule, wars and pestilence took their toll on Nîmes. Its fortunes revived for a while with the textile industry. Sturdy fabric with indigo dye was fabricated into laborers' clothes and became known as "denim" (*de Nîmes*). It was exported via Genoa, which led to the nickname "jeans."

The covered market opened in 1885 in a high-ceilinged structure of steel and glass that evoked the Baltard style of the Parisian covered markets. Regrettably, that structure was dismantled. The new building lacks charm, but it remains a popular destination for regional products.

La Fromagerie Vergne's selection includes Pélardon, a small round goat's-milk cheese with a nutty, peppery tang from goats grazing in the Cévennes mountains of Languedoc.

The *département* of Gard is known for crunchy, green Picholine olives. Olives Daniel sells them, as well as oils made from a blend of olives but dominated by Picholine. The anchovy spread and tapenades are also excellent. *Brandade de Nîmes* is salt cod that has been poached in milk and then mashed with olive oil and garlic. The creamy purée has a surprisingly smooth, mild flavor. *Petit pâté nîmois,* a pastry pie stuffed with veal and pork, is best eaten hot. Thierry Bosc sells them and other delicacies such as bull meat from the Camargue. *Croquant Villaret,* a hard biscuit, is made according to a recipe that dates from 1775. For a treat that's easier to sink your teeth into, try the *caladon* with almonds and honey.

On Friday morning Nîmes hosts a farmers' market on Allées Jaurès on the western side of town. The market occurs year-round, though it shrinks during winter when the fields are slumbering. If you have time after the market, walk to Les Jardins de la Fontaine, grandly designed gardens with fountains and children's activities.

Lambesc

⚜ SMALL PROVENÇAL MARKET ⚜

WHEN: *Friday morning*

WHERE: *Village center*

THE EARTHQUAKE OF 1909 did damage to this village, but the houses and fountains that withstood the tremblors bear testament to a prosperous past. One of the village's most striking features—both literally and figuratively—is the Jacquemard clock. Four figures strike the bells every quarter hour, though no one seems to hurry at the morning market. Shoppers rest baskets bulging with cabbage, apples, cheese, and bread at their feet as they catch up with the latest news.

Pertuis

· TRADITIONAL PROVENÇAL MARKET ·

WHEN: *Friday morning*

WHERE: *Town center*

ERTUIS IS THE GATEWAY to the Luberon for those coming from Aix or Marseille. The town has a 13th-century bell tower and old fountains whose gurgling waters soften the clamor of the market. Sellers cater to the needs and means of local residents. Merchandise is utilitarian (lots of underwear and children's clothing), vendors are friendly, and prices are attractive. Plump figs and cantaloupes tempt in summertime. Cheeses, *saucissons,* and rotisserie chicken make it easy to assemble a full meal. *Tourtons du champsaur,* dough stuffed with potatoes, spinach, or cheese, are a specialty of the Hautes-Alpes. On Wednesday and Saturday mornings during the growing season there's a farmers' market on Place Garcin. For a wine and garden tour, visit the lovely Château Val Joanis.

Terroir

Terroir refers to the land and the unique qualities that soil chemistry and growing conditions contribute to the flavor of what grows there. Human know-how, or *savoir-faire,* also shapes the outcome. *Terroir* is rooted in the belief that wine and food are shaped by their total environment. Slight variations can have a big impact: All Provençal goat cheeses don't taste the same, nor do all Provençal olive oils or wines. Indeed, the same *Mourvèdre* grape grown on different parcels of land—even adjacent parcels—can produce wines with different characteristics.

Ask any French person about *terroir* and you're likely to trigger a fervent response. Locals seem to be born with a food memory that enables them to distinguish the authenticity of *terroir* as they sip a full-bodied Rhône wine or swallow a warm, runny bite of black truffle omelet. The rest of us might never acquire that sixth sense, but we'll surely enjoy trying.

What's for Lunch?

Most Provençal markets start closing at lunchtime. Many shoppers head to a café or restaurant to refuel. There's always one, sometimes several, close to the market that offers a *formule,* meaning you pick two or three courses from a preset menu. For many travelers to Provence, *le pique-nique* stands out as the favorite meal of the trip. These items are available at the markets and require no preparation.

❧ Breads—Fresh breads include *pain aux céréales* (whole grain with seeds) or *pain complet* (wheat bread). If you don't find a loaf that appeals at the market, the local *boulangerie* is usually open until noon.

❧ Cheeses—Goat cheese rounds are convenient for picnics. *Fromageries* at the market or in the village have a broader selection; you can request *une petite tranche* of a firm Comté, a blue-veined Roquefort, or a slightly salty *tomme de Savoie.*

❧ *Saucissons*—Dried sausages come in pork, venison, boar, and other varieties. Slice thinly and put atop buttered bread.

- Olives—Ask for a handful (*une bonne poignée*) of black olives from Nyons or the green Lucques or Picholines.

- Tapenades—Black and green olive spreads are available at olive stands, or branch out to try anchovy or eggplant.

- Vegetables—Carrots, cucumbers, tomatoes, and radishes are just a few that are delicious raw.

- Fruits—Pick whatever is freshest of the season, perhaps strawberries, cherries, apricots, figs, or grapes.

- Pâtés and salads—*Traiteurs* or *charcuteries* sell *pâté de campagne* and prepared salads such as celery root in a smooth mayonnaise sauce (*céleri rémoulade*).

- Pizza—Made to order in wood-fired ovens on trucks; local favorites are anchovy and olive toppings.

- Paella—Saffron-flavored rice, shellfish, and sausage.

- Asian food—Noodles, egg rolls, and other specialties.

- Rotisserie meats—Roasted chicken, turkey legs, rabbit, and quail are sometimes options.

- Dessert—Cookies or nougats, or stop at a local *pâtisserie* for an *éclair* or fruit *tarte*.

- A folding knife might come in handy, as well as a corkscrew. You can often find those at the markets, too!

Saturday

· MARKETS ·

Best

Apt *(traditional Provençal market)*

Arles *(traditional Provençal market)*

Uzès *(traditional Provençal market)*

Villeneuve-lèz-Avignon *(flea/antiques market)*

Aix-en-Provence *(traditional Provençal market)*, see p. 151

Avignon *(covered market)*, see p. 161

Velleron *(farmers' market)*, see p. 133

Others

Le Thor *(traditional Provençal market)*

Pernes-les-Fontaines *(traditional Provençal market)*

Nîmes *(covered market)*, see p. 213

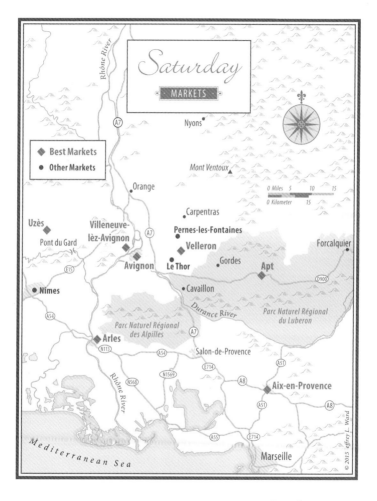

Saturday
MARKETS

Rhône River

Nyons

Mont Ventoux

◆ Best Markets
● Other Markets

Orange

Carpentras

Uzès
Pont du Gard

Villeneuve-
lèz-Avignon

Pernes-les-Fontaines

Velleron

Forcalquier

Avignon

Le Thor

Gordes

Apt

● Nimes

Cavaillon

Durance River

Parc Naturel Régional
du Luberon

Parc Naturel Régional
des Alpilles

Arles

Salon-de-Provence

Rhône River

Aix-en-Provence

Mediterranean Sea

Marseille

© 2015 Jeffrey L. Ward

Apt

TRADITIONAL PROVENÇAL MARKET

WHEN: *Saturday morning*

WHERE: *Town center*

OFFICE DE TOURISME: *20 Avenue Philippe Girard,*
84400 Apt. Tel: 04.90.74.03.18. www.luberon-apt.fr

EVER SINCE THE ROMANS colonized it in AD 300, Apt has been a center of commerce. It sits astride the Via Domitia, the oldest road in France, which stretches from Rome through Nîmes to Narbonnes near the Spanish border. The market dates to the 12th century, when Apt was ruled by counts and bishops who controlled different sections of town and competed with each other for the best market. In high season there are about 350 stalls; during off-season, about half that number.

Sellers were originally grouped by type. Meat vendors, for example, gathered at Place de la Bouquerie. But now all types of vendors are mixed together. One way to navigate this market is to start at Place de la Bouquerie, on the western edge of the *centre ville,* and wend your way eastward. At Place Gabriel Péri, near the town hall, the square throbs with activity. Walk up the elegant stairway, which leads to the regional government office (*sous-préfecture*), for a view of the rainbow of umbrellas shading the market stands. Continue on Rue des Marchands to Place du

Postel and Place Jean Jaurès, then onward to Rue Saint-Pierre and Place Lauze de Perret. Don't worry about the names; if you follow the flow of shoppers you'll see most of the stands as you weave a crooked path through the town.

Apt's sprawling market is one of my favorites. Excitement fills the air from early morning until the market's close. Plenty of tourists visit, but this market draws mainly locals from Apt and from surrounding villages in the Luberon. It helps that it's on a Saturday, when most villagers aren't working but are anticipating a big family meal on Sunday. There's lots of socializing. Market shopping Provençal style is never a chore.

Produce vendors sell radishes that were recently pulled from the ground, and Savoy cabbages big as basketballs. Apricots, cherries, and strawberries are at a perfect pitch of ripeness. Other stalls feature local wines, salamis, spices and herbs, and breads. Fresh-cut flowers make a fine centerpiece for the traditional Sunday meal, and many shoppers choose a bouquet before they leave. Nougat candies, olive oils, local honeys, and fruit jams won't disappoint either. For the health conscious, *petit-épeautre* (a nutritious grain that's grown locally at higher altitudes) can be purchased inexpensively.

Fresh goat cheeses attract a line of customers. I wait my turn to buy a *chèvre* that's semi-dry. When the vendor asks, *"Avec ceci?"* (And what else?), I can't resist and point to a Banon wrapped in chestnut leaves. In fact, I already bought a Banon cheese from another vendor where I paid almost double the price. As I take stock of the three cheeses in my basket, I'm reminded not to buy the first items that tempt me. It's better to scope out the market and

then decide what looks best. A good indicator is where lines are longest—that's usually a tip-off to where the locals prefer to shop.

Some olive vendors buy marinated olives from wholesalers. But the flavor and freshness of olives from a *confiserie artisanale d'olives,* whose olive preparations they've made themselves, are incomparably better. There's also no shortage of prepared foods, such as baked-to-order pizzas, Asian egg rolls and noodles, and chicken that's been turning on a rotisserie.

Rue des Marchands is filled with market vendors, shops, and historic sites. The Cathedral Sainte-Anne, built in the 12th century, is supposedly where Mary's mother was buried, which made it a stop along the pilgrimage routes. Most market tables belong to independent vendors, but some are extensions of the shops behind them. Admiring the bright blooms at one stand, I ask the seller where he gets the plants. He drives to Carpentras at 3 a.m. to buy them from a trusted wholesaler.

The almost-lost art of basketmaking is alive and well at Nicolas Appel's stand. He weaves by hand, without glue, using willow branches that he grows in Beaumont-de-Pertuis. His baskets are both beautiful and practical. Each design has a different name— *glacier, plateau au fromage, fraise*—which describes what it was originally designed to carry. His son is learning to weave, so the skill may pass to the next generation. Another artist sells sand paintings. She and her husband developed a technique for coloring sand with pigments from the local ochre.

A *traiteur* from Roussillon sells homemade *patés* and terrines in tins. Pork sprinkled with lavender is popular. In Place du Postrel, another goat-cheese seller does a brisk business. Her farm in Saignan is called La Cabriole, or "goat" in the old Provençal language.

Even when the Apt market gets crowded, it maintains a relaxed ambience. Musicians serenade shoppers and hope for a few coins. Vendors are cheerful and patient. An oysterman gives me a detailed explanation of their sizes and shapes and where they come from. A woman selling napkins that she has sewn herself instructs me how to wash them, even though other customers are waiting in line.

A concentration of Arab vendors and halal butchers fills the Place des Martyrs de la Résistance. This part of the market has its own distinct personality. Business moves briskly, and it's noisier. There's a lot of produce, usually at lower prices than elsewhere in the market. Vendors shout *"Allez-y, Allez, Allez!"* to call customers to their tables. Muslim women in traditional dress fill boxes with produce while the men cluster in conversations.

Passing through the ancient wall and crossing over to Place Lauze de Perret, there's another hub of market activity. As soon as one exits the pedestrian zone, a rumble of car and motorcycle engines assaults the ears. Stalls sell mass-produced clothing, accessories, soaps, and some food. The quality is uneven, but the prices are low.

Don't leave Apt without trying their local specialty, *fruits confits* (sugar-preserved fruits). They aren't sold at the market because they don't hold up in outdoor conditions. But they're worth seeking out in one of the shops that still make them by the traditional method, such as Confiserie Le Coulon and Confiserie Marcel

Richaud (see p. 157.) Other local treats include homemade lavender ice cream at Au Pierrot Blanc and ochre nougats at Pâtisserie J. C. Roussett, both on Rue des Marchands.

Several *boulangeries* sell *pain de Luberon* made with *blé meunier d'Apt,* flour that's ground from an old variety of local grain. The line of customers extends out the door on Rue Saint-Pierre at the bakery Le Saint-Pierre. Butcher shops, such as Chez Malavard, offer wild game in the fall, and *patés* and prepared side dishes all year-round. La Cave du Septier, on Place du Septier, has an impressive selection of well-priced wines. For books and maps, Fontaine Luberon at 16 Rue des Marchands is a good stop.

Earthenware pottery is another local specialty. In the 18th century, ceramics were a major part of the economy as potters were drawn to the red clay. The area still attracts artisans. You can pick up a brochure with addresses of ceramic studios from the Office de Tourisme.

The market starts to wind down around noon. By 1 p.m., the vendors' attention shifts to disassembling their stalls and packing up their vans. A gleaner pedals by on a bicycle. He grabs a melon from a pile of trash seconds before the sanitation trucks pull in with engines roaring and hoses poised. The streets will be swept clean in a matter of minutes. All traces of this lively market will disappear . . . until next Saturday morning rolls around, with renewed anticipation and replenished stalls.

Chef Fabricio Delgaudio

Brazilian-born chef Fabricio Delgaudio opened Le Sanglier Paresseux (the Lazy Boar) in 2009 in Caseneuve,
a quiet hilltop perch overlooking the Luberon. It's a
tucked-away gem of a restaurant within easy driving distance of Apt.

Chef Delgaudio has olive-colored skin, wavy black hair,
and dark, penetrating eyes. He smiles often, and it spreads
to others as he circulates among the tables, chatting with
customers as if surrounded by friends. Delgaudio started
cooking in Brazil at the age of 16. He traveled to France to
study in Lyon, trained with Alain Ducasse and with Yannick Alléno at Le Meurice in Paris, and had a restaurant
in Lisbon. After falling in love with a woman from the
Luberon, they moved to be near her family.

"What I love about cooking in France is that it's a
passion both for the chefs and for the clients," he says. He
uses Brazilian spices and know-how to accent the foods
of his adopted homeland. "In other places, cooking is all
about the business," he says. "But here it's about the food.
The guests are my engine. They keep me going and drive
my passion." His aim is that they will have a smile on
their faces when they leave.

Local, seasonal produce dictates the menu. Each course is a dynamic combination of flavors, colors, and textures. Some details are simple—sprinkles of red pepper flakes or a single purple-veined leaf of lettuce—but add flourishes far out of proportion to their size. Others are more complicated, such as a dessert with "mushrooms" made of chocolate stems and rounded white meringue tops. After lunch, I leave with a smile, and so does everyone else.

Le Sanglier Paresseux is at 84750 Caseneuve. Tel: 04.90.75.17.70. www.sanglierparesseux.com

Arles

WHEN: *Saturday and Wednesday mornings*
(Saturday market is larger)

WHERE: *Boulevard des Lices and Boulevard Émile Combe*

OFFICE DE TOURISME: *Boulevard des Lices,*
13200 Arles. Tel: 04.90.18.41.20. www.arlestourisme.com

*A*RLES IS A HUB for Provençal culture. Efforts to preserve the Provençal language find many supporters here, and festivals provide opportunities for locals to pull out their traditional Arlesian costumes. Every three years a new Queen of Arles is elected to be the guardian of Provençal culture, dress, and language.

The city's heritage as a major trading post is due in part to its location on the Rhône River near the sea. The emperors Julius Caesar and, later, Augustus cherished Arles. Its influence grew with the expansion of the Roman Empire as veterans of military campaigns settled here. The Roman theater at the top of a hill was completed in 10 BC. It's a distinctive sight with two marble columns still standing. A two-tiered Roman arena was built to accommodate 20,000 spectators as they cheered chariot races or gruesome hand-to-hand combats. It still draws crowds for bullfighting festivals and other performances.

Arles is also a prominent center for the arts. For many, it's indelibly associated with Van Gogh, who lived and painted in Arles during one of the most prolific periods of his career. It's celebrated for Les Rencontres d'Arles, a major annual international photography festival. Among fashionistas, it may be best known as the birthplace of designer Christian Lacroix.

The vibrant market is one of the city's proudest and longest-standing traditions. With its prime location near the Mediterranean Sea and surrounded by the fertile Rhône valley, the Arles market offers a wide assortment of fish, produce, olives and oils, and other items. The market's scale (it extends over 2 km) and

ambience are very different from the small village markets, though both have a place in the mix. Saturday is the biggest and best market day, although the smaller Wednesday market is significant enough to warrant a visit.

My favorite part of the Saturday market is the local producers' section (*marché paysan*) near the Office de Tourisme. Fruits and vegetables, rice, cheeses and yogurts, honeys, fig and apricot jams, and other delicacies are at their freshest. If organic is important to you, look for the AB (*Agriculture Biologique*) sign. Monsieur Chabert has apples, pressed juices, and olive oils from his farm,

Grand Mas du Roy. A baker pulls warm loaves of bread from a canvas sack to restock his table. A sheep farmer brings lamb and mutton. Across the aisle, a woman displays local pork products under the sign Gallician.

Beyond the specially designated *marché paysan* area are other high-quality stands. Fromagerie Roumanille sells local goat cheeses, as well as a sweet and nutty Comté from cows that graze in the mountains of the Haut-Vaucluse. If olives are your thing (and they should be while you're in Provence), the olives and tapenades at the Gautier stand are fresh and flavorful.

I had the privilege of touring the Arles market with Michelin-starred chef Jean-Luc Rabanel who introduced me to several of his favorite vendors and items. He pointed out *tellines*, small clams that are native to the waters of the Mediterranean near Arles. They offer the tiniest sliver of meat, but it's sweet and mellow. *Telline* fishermen are a breed unto themselves. They wade deep in the water dragging a net through the sand. It can take five hours of trolling to capture only ten kilos of *tellines*. Other Mediterranean fish were also harvested early that morning: *le violet de roche* (known as the prickly sea potato because of its shape), pointy-tipped snails (*escargots pointus*), and several varieties of oysters. (For more on my market tour with Chef Rabanel, see p. 242.)

The Arles market has a great variety of goods. Flower vendors along Boulevard des Lices sell big bunches of sunflowers and pink peonies. Immigrant vendors sell inexpensive clothing and household basics along Boulevard Émile Combes where sections of ancient stone ramparts are visible behind the stalls. The items can be a salvation; I need shoelaces and manage to find some here.

Arles is known for sausages. However, most *saucissons d'Arles* at markets throughout Provence are not really made in Arles. To taste the sausage at its most authentic, visit the shop La Farandole–Maison Genin (11 Rue des Porcelets). Bernard Genin, a fifth-generation sausage maker, follows the original recipe, developed in the 1600s. It includes pork and beef, red wine, garlic, and peppercorns, and ages for two months until it reaches perfection. Bernard and his wife, Brigitte, produce about 100 of these peppery sausages each week.

Other shops with local products include La Cave des Saveurs (25 Rue des Suisses) for regional foods, Fadoli (46 Rue des Arènes) for olive oils, and La Fromagerie Arlésienne (6 Place Antonelle) for cheeses. L'Arlésienne (on Rue du Président Wilson) specializes in local costumes. Indiennes de Nîmes (14 Place de la République) has cowboy clothing in the Camargue tradition. Both Souleiado and Les Olivades (No. 10 and No. 4 on Boulevard des Lices) sell splendid clothing and fabrics in Provençal colors.

If shopping leaves you hungry, several restaurants emphasize local ingredients. Or find simpler refreshment at the Bar du Marché or other cafés on Boulevard des Lices where you can enjoy *l'art de vivre* like a true Arlesian.

The first Wednesday of each month, Arles also hosts a sizable flea and antiques market (see p. 136).

Chef Jean-Luc Rabanel

Jean-Luc Rabanel received his first Michelin star in 1999, which was followed by two more stars and other accolades. He was one of the first French chefs to feature organic ingredients. Rabanel creates dishes with subtlety and finesse. Dabs of colorful sauces adorn the plates like semiprecious stones. Other dishes are strewn with edible flowers.

Rabanel is passionate about cooking with the local bounty. He sources some ingredients from the market in Arles and allows me to tag along one Saturday morning. He has a broad build and strong hands—the physique of a man accustomed to physical labor. It's easy to follow his mane of blond hair as he moves through the crowd like a lion, exuding confidence in his command of the terrain.

He heads straight to the *marché paysan,* where local producers recognize the chef and smile proudly if he pauses at their stands. Regarding the *tellines,* clams tiny as fingernails, he says, "All they need is a quick sauté with olive oil, garlic, and parsley." *Poisson bleu, violet de roche, moules de pleine mer, and soupe de roche* are used in traditional Provençal soup though challenging to catch. He describes the fishermen in admiring tones.

"Always go first to the local growers' market stalls because their items are better," he advises. To emphasize the point he adds, "Don't mix the napkins with the rags." I look at him quizzically, and he explains: "We use a napkin to wipe the mouth and a rag to clean floors. It's important not to confuse them."

Chef Rabanel halts abruptly when unusual tomato plants catch his eye. He calls his restaurant and asks some-

one to pick up a few for his organic garden. As we pass a mountain of garlic, he whispers, "The quantity that we use in our cooking is *incroyable*!" He pinches the stem of a zucchini blossom and twirls it under his nose as he inhales its delicate aroma. His eyes sparkle with the excitement of an artist in a hurry to return to his studio—and our market tour is over.

L'Atelier de Jean-Luc Rabanel is at 7 Rue des Carmes, 13200 Arles. Tel: 04.90.91.07.69. The casual Le Bistrot à Coté is at 21 Rue des Carmes. Tel: 04.90.97.61.13. www.rabanel.com

Uzès

WHEN: *Saturday morning*

WHERE: *Town center*

OFFICE DE TOURISME: *Chapelle des Capucins, Place Albert 1er, 30700 Uzès. Tel: 04.66.22.68.88. www.uzes-tourisme.com*

Uzès LIES WEST of the Rhône River in the Languedoc region. Although it falls slightly outside this book's geographical focus, its exceptional market is too good to omit. Day trippers from Avignon, Arles, and Nîmes visit Uzès for a change of scenery and a chance to stroll a market in a beautiful setting. As one friend describes the experience, "We don't just shop at the market—we breathe it in."

Perched on a hill, Uzès overlooks the limestone cliffs and gorges of the Eure valley. En route you might pass the Pont du Gard, an aqueduct over the Gard River that was built by the Romans in the 1st century BC and has been designated a UNESCO World Heritage site. Proximity to the river ensured Uzès a supply of water and with it, prosperity. Textile, silk, and hosiery production became major industries. But mulberry disease and competition took their toll, and the town's distance from major highways and TGV rail lines hastened the downward spiral of its economy. Recently, however, Uzès has been climbing back to greatness. The old town has been beautifully restored, thanks to redevelopment funds put to good use. Music and dance festivals bring a steady influx of creative energy.

But more than anything else, it's the Saturday market that has contributed to the town's rejuvenation. After the main plazas were renovated, access streets widened, and Renaissance buildings returned to their splendor, this market's popularity soared. Now, at the height of the season, about 200 vendors bring their best wares to sell at this market, attracting large numbers of locals and tourists. There's a waiting list of vendors who would like the chance to participate.

One can find everything that evokes Provence at this market, from floral-patterned fabrics to local wines and cheeses, seasonal produce, fragrant herbs, and flowers. Starting in April, the produce stalls fill with asparagus and strawberries. Come summertime, there are cherries, apricots, tomatoes, and melons. By autumn, it's pumpkins and squashes. And in winter, black truffles add excitement to the usual offerings.

A festive spirit infuses the Uzès market. One Saturday, accordion players parade around the stalls, pausing just long enough to hand out leaflets promoting an accordion festival. During the Fête du Pois Chiche (yes, a chickpea festival) a character dressed in silky yellow shorts, a black turtleneck, a taffeta cape, and headgear that looks remarkably like a masked chickpea darts through the crowd creating excitement. Uzès always seems to be having a party of one kind or another.

Market activity buzzes at Place aux Herbes in the heart of the town. The square is lined with graceful arcades and anchored by a fountain. The lively market continues in Place Dampmartin and along Rue Jacques d'Uzès and Rue de la République. Sister Ambrosiac sells heavenly marmalades, wines, and honeys made by nuns at the Solan Monastery. *Croquille bourguignonne* at Cyril Santos's stand is snail meat seasoned with garlic and herbs, stuffed into pastry biscuits that resemble snail shells. Fresh Mediterranean fish at Poissonnerie Clément glisten atop a bed of ice.

Le Moulin d'Uzès has won medals for its olive oils, a notable accomplishment since it began production only a few years ago. Olive oil made from *Picholine de Nîmes* is smooth and peppery. Miu Païs sells *crème d'asperges* and other homemade sauces. At Nom d'un Pistil, a woman sells saffron and lavender in various forms. She explains that it takes 150 saffron flowers to yield a single gram of saffron threads, and that saffron syrup adds a special touch to white wine or champagne for an *apéritif.* I'm happy to find a vendor selling *fougasse d'Aigues-Mortes,* a flat bread made with brioche dough, orange essence, sugar, and salt from the Camargue. Annie, a goat-cheese maker, adorns round cheeses with tiny orange calendula blossoms. She also sells aged goat cheeses that she calls *les introuvables.* If you grate them atop salads and other dishes, they'll add a robust accent similar to Parmesan.

Uzès has numerous boutiques with unique items. Galleries display local pottery, a specialty of the region. (To see more, take a short drive to the pottery village Saint-Quentin-les-Poteries.) There's also a choice of cafés and restaurants. La Fille des Vignes, well situated next to a fountain on Place Albert, serves simple hearty fare such as *charcuterie* platters and lamb casserole. For tapas made with organic produce, Les Terroirs offers delicious options, including items from the market, such as Cyril Santos's *escargots.* Its outdoor terrace makes a comfortable perch for watching the market at Place aux Herbes wind down to closing time. The accordion players make a final pass through the cobbled streets, sending music like bright balloons into the clear blue Provençal sky.

Villeneuve-lèz-Avignon

❧ FLEA AND ANTIQUES MARKET ❧

WHEN: *Saturday morning, 6 a.m.–1 p.m.*

WHERE: *Place Charles David*

OFFICE DE TOURISME: *Place Charles David,
30400 Villeneuve-lèz-Avignon. Tel: 04.90.25.61.33.
www.ot-villeneuvelezavignon.fr*

ONLY A STONE'S THROW across the Rhône River from Avignon, Villeneuve-lèz-Avignon is off the beaten path and yet easily within reach of those who know it's worth a visit. Wealthy cardinals were on to this in the 14th century, when they chose to build palatial residences here rather than in crowded Avignon, the papal seat during that period. Local monuments bear the imprint of a rich history. Fort Saint-André, a towering stronghold built in the 14th century, guarded the border of France when Avignon was allied to the Holy Roman Empire. Both it and the Philippe le Bel tower offer views of the countryside.

Villeneuve's flea and antiques market is not as well known as the one in L'Isle-sur-la-Sorgue, but that only adds to its appeal. For those familiar with the flea markets in Paris, one could loosely compare the Sunday market in L'Isle-sur-la-Sorgue to the Marché aux Puces de Saint-Ouen (also known as Clignancourt). The smaller Saturday market in Villeneuve is similar to the Marché aux

Puces de la Porte de Vanves in Paris. All are great markets, though some shoppers prefer the smaller ones. They have fewer dealers, but they attract fewer customers and improve the chances of finding great deals. They're also easy to cover in their entirety during a short outing. I've heard it said of both Clignancourt and L'Isle-sur-la-Sorgue that dealers make their rounds to the smaller markets to snap up the best items and then resell them at a profit. Regardless, the quality is decent and the prices are fair at Villeneuve's flea market. Savvy shoppers arrive early for the best selection.

Roughly 80 vendors set out their wares on blankets or folding tables in a parking lot in view of Fort Saint-André. Dishes, linens, and decorative tins will tickle the fancy of some collectors. Fruit-wood printing blocks, wine barrels, and garden furnishings will beckon others. Walnut tables and bureaus reflect the morning sun off their polished patinas. Small wooden cages, called *panetières,* are intended for mounting on walls to store bread and keep out rodents. Tables for kneading dough, their surfaces worn from use, are also typical of Provençal furniture. Linen napkins are large enough to cover small side tables. The dealer explains that they were sized to protect women's dresses that billowed at their laps with many folds of fabric. I'm sure there are other explanations, but this one satisfies my curiosity.

Santons catch my eye, clay figurines (or occasionally wood) decorated to represent traditional Provençal trades. So, too, do *pastis* glasses, old wheelbarrows, mismatched terra-cotta floor tiles, and window shutters so faded and peeling they are quintessentially

Provençal. As always at flea markets, some items delight by their shock value, such as a large goblet engraved "cocaine."

The vendors are professionals, not individuals clearing unwanted items from their attics such as you find at *vide-greniers*. They have their private sources and attend estate sales to replenish their stock. Most don't speak much English, but they'll do their best to help you understand the merchandise. I saw a vendor lift a cane-seat chair and throw it down to demonstrate that it was well made and durable. Prices are reasonable, although there is room for respectful bargaining. Don't expect huge reductions, but enough for the purchase to conclude on a happy note.

Midmorning, three sellers gather around a table, where they spread an antique linen cloth. They pull out food and a bottle of wine while keeping a casual eye on their merchandise in case a serious customer comes by. Vendors selling hot chocolate, croissants, and oysters ensure that no shoppers go hungry or thirsty.

Poke around the village after you've visited the market. The Carthusian monastery Chartreuse du Val de Bénédiction, founded in the 14th century by Pope Innocent VI, is one of France's largest. You can walk among the cloisters, visit the monks' cells, and stroll in the gardens. Such a tranquil setting, and yet it's within close range of Avignon. Those cardinals knew what they were doing when they picked this little corner of heaven.

Other Highlights

I'm a hardcore fan of markets as a way to explore local culture and cuisine. But even I can't tolerate a diet of markets every day. I sprinkle in other activities as a cultural palate cleanser. Here are some favorites.

Picturesque Villages

It's rare for a village or town not to have its own market, but several hold interest even with no market to recommend them. Climb the ancient streets of the perched village of Lacoste to the ruins of the *château* where the Marquis de Sade lived, and take in views across the valley to Bonnieux. Les Baux-de-Provence has the Carrière de Lumières, a sound-and-light show inside a quarry that's wildly popular. Oppède-le-Vieux is another example of an abandoned village, a mere shadow of its former self, but it holds historical interest if you're willing to make the steep climb to a church and ruins of a castle amid a thicket of brambles. Crillon-le-Brave, near Bédoin, is a relaxing refuge atop a hill with views of Mont Ventoux and a superb Relais & Châteaux inn. The village of Buoux, high in the Luberon, has the remains of a castle, a fort, and caves that are rich with prehistoric meaning. Fontaine-de-Vaucluse rewards visitors with its natural spring (the source of the Sorgue River) and waterside cafés.

Historical and Architectural Highlights

Provence has some of the world's best preserved Roman ruins in and near Arles, Nîmes, Orange, Vaison-la-Romaine, and Saint-Rémy. Other hallmarks of local architecture are belfries and public fountains. Wrought-iron cages that house church bells might look fragile, but they're designed to allow the mistral's gusts to blow through without damage. Nowadays nearly every household has running water, but in earlier times the public fountains were the closest source of water. Elaborately designed fountains, such as in Aix-en-Provence, were ways that townspeople celebrated and boasted of their good fortune.

The Camargue

The large nature preserve at the delta of the Rhône River is an enchanting sight with wild white horses and pink flamingoes roaming a vast expanse of scrubby wetlands. The sky dips so low that it seems to caress the earth. The surreal landscape has to be experienced to be believed. For a memorable adventure, make arrangements with one of the ranches to explore it on horseback. *(continued)*

Wine Tours

You don't have to be an aficionado or have your own wine cellar to enjoy the area's celebrated vineyards. If you tour them with an experienced guide, you'll learn a lot and visit lesser-known wineries.

Biking and Hiking

It's easy to rent bicycles or follow well-marked hiking trails to explore the countryside. Tourist offices can provide information. A host of tour operators offer Provence itineraries. If you go on a group tour, I recommend extending your stay by a couple of days for more market explorations.

Theme Tours

Cooking classes, garden visits, and wine tours are among the many ways to explore the area through a particular lens. Travel planning services such as Julie Mautner's Provence Post can help you design the vacation of your dreams.

· OTHER SATURDAY MARKETS ·

· SMALL PROVENÇAL MARKET ·

WHEN: *Saturday morning (and a smaller one on Wednesday)*

WHERE: *Place du Marché*

LE THOR'S market covers the basics: cheese, meat, honey, bread, produce, fish, and furniture repair. The Sorgue River flows past the town, cooling it during summer and, in years past, powering the mills that converted plants into dyes. Synthetics replaced natural dyes, and the mills are gone. But public architecture adds some interest: The nave of the Romanesque church is spanned by the oldest Gothic vaulted ceiling in Provence. The waters of the Sorgue practically lap at the base of the church, giving it the appearance of a stone ship that has set its anchor for all time. Porte de Douzabas supports a clock tower crowned with a campanile resembling an onion. It is the only remnant of the ramparts that once surrounded the town.

Another attraction in Le Thor is antiques shops along the road to L'Isle-sur-la-Sorgue. Brocante Altiero, for example, sells garden statuary, furniture, and lighting. Massive cast-iron antelopes, bulls, and roosters might give you reason to pause.

Pernes-les-Fontaines

WHEN: *Saturday morning*

WHERE: *Quai de Verdun*

MIDWAY BETWEEN L'Isle-sur-la-Sorgue and Carpentras lies a little village with a big treasure—water. The village celebrates its natural springs with 40 public fountains. Some are discreetly tucked into corners, while others are massive carved sculptures.

The water supports a robust farming tradition, and the season's bounty is available at the market: cherries, strawberries, asparagus, and melons. On Saturday locals stock up and socialize with their neighbors. Pernes also has a Wednesday evening farmers' market from spring through fall and a craft market on Friday evening in July and August. On July 14, France's Independence Day, Pernes-les-Fontaines exalts the local *Cavaillon* melons with a Fête du Melon. Farmers offer tastes and give tips on how to select the sweetest, juiciest ones.

For a special meal in Pernes, try Au Fil du Temps. The chef finds imaginative ways of working with local ingredients. The restaurant is located in a pretty square with—you guessed it—a trickling fountain.

More Options

Farther North Villages

A N IMAGINARY LINE connecting Orange, Bédoin, and Sault marks the northern boundary of this book's geographical focus—except for Vaison-la-Romaine and Nyons, market towns of such importance that their inclusion is essential. Other villages beckon with excellent Côtes du Rhône wines and outdoor activities. If you venture in that direction, here are a few suggestions.

BUIS-LES-BARONNIES (*Wednesday morning market*)

Market offerings include local goat cheeses, olives, Muscat grapes, lavender, saffron, and *tilleul* (linden) leaves. Colorful façades and Gothic arcades add interest to this village in the Drôme, which also attracts rock climbers to scale the Rocher Saint-Julien.

CAIRANNE

The village no longer has a weekly market; however, it is well regarded for its full-bodied red wines. They are designated Côtes du Rhône Villages AOC (a step up from Côtes du Rhône AOC without "Villages"), and Cairanne is permitted to add its name to the label, which signifies even greater desirability.

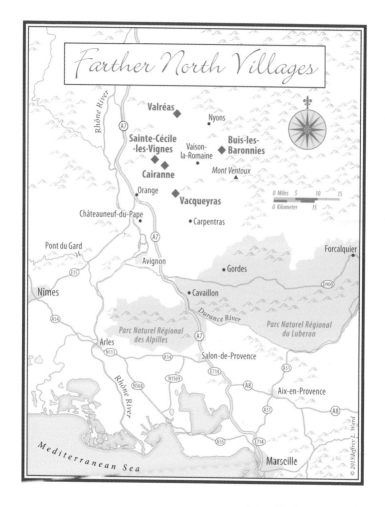

Farther North Villages

Rhône River

Valréas

Nyons

Sainte-Cécile -les-Vignes

Vaison-la-Romaine

Buis-les-Baronnies

Cairanne

Mont Ventoux

Orange

Vacqueyras

Châteauneuf-du-Pape

Carpentras

Pont du Gard

Avignon

Gordes

Forcalquier

Nîmes

Cavaillon

Durance River

Parc Naturel Régional du Luberon

Parc Naturel Régional des Alpilles

Arles

Salon-de-Provence

Aix-en-Provence

Rhône River

Mediterranean Sea

Marseille

0 Miles 5 10 15
0 Kilometer 15

© 2015 Jeffrey L. Ward

SAINTE-CÉCILE-LES-VIGNES *(Saturday morning market)*

This village in the heart of Côtes du Rhône wine country has a good market. Specialties include olives, cheeses, honeys, herbs and spices, and fresh produce. A bust of Baron Le Roy pays tribute to the man credited with creating the AOC (Appellation d'Origine Côntrollée) system for classifying French wines.

VACQUEYRAS *(Thursday morning market)*

The village market is not a standout, but its wines are. Local grapes produce one of the most important appellations of the Côtes du Rhône and earned Vacqueyras its own designation. A peppery blend made from Grenache and Syrah grapes reflects the *terroir*. The nearby village of Gigondas also produces a highly regarded wine.

VALRÉAS *(Wednesday morning market)*

As a market town, Valréas is most interesting during truffle season (November–March), when the coveted "black diamonds" (*Tuber melanosporum*) come into season. Valréas is part of the Enclave des Papes, territory that belonged to the papacy in the 14th century. Legend goes that the pope fell ill while visiting Valréas, but his condition improved after he was offered local wine as a remedy. He purchased the land to ensure an ongoing supply and later supplemented it by adding the surrounding villages.

Nice and Other Mediterranean Markets

NICE *(Daily markets)*

Neither Frédéric Mistral nor Jean Giono, defenders of Provençal culture, considered Nice to be "real" Provence. History has shaped it as more Italian than French. But as a market city, anyone would be proud to claim it. Market stalls with candy-striped awnings take over Cours Saleya, surrounded by Italianate buildings painted shades that bring to mind fruit sorbets. Tuesday through Sunday mornings, vendors' crates brim with vegetables and fruits, cheeses, olives, *saucissons,* and much more. *Socca,* a local specialty, is a *crêpe* made with chickpea flour. Dazzling flowers can be purchased at reasonable prices. The food market is open until 1 p.m.; the flower market remains open until 5:30 p.m. (1 p.m. on Sundays). Every Monday from 7 a.m. to 6 p.m., Cours Saleya transforms into a large flea market where vendors sell old French lace, linens, silver, and furniture. Additionally, Nice hosts a craft market from June to September, starting at 6 p.m. daily, and a rotating cycle of markets on Saturdays near the Palais de Justice; a book market on the first and third Saturday of every month; paintings and crafts on the second Saturday; and vintage postcards and prints on the fourth.

SAINT-TROPEZ *(Tuesday and Saturday morning markets)*

Brigitte Bardot gets credit for rocketing this town to fame after filming the beach scenes in *And God Created Woman,* directed by Roger Vadim. As popular as Saint-Tropez is with the well-heeled set, its twice-weekly market keeps faith with Provençal simplicity. Century-old plane trees divide the space into generous *allées.* Food, flowers, clothing, and jewelry abound. Shoppers stock up on provisions to take to the beach or to the tiny harbor where enormous yachts anchor cheek by jowl.

CASSIS *(Wednesday and Friday morning markets)*

Frédéric Mistral said, "He who has seen Paris but not Cassis has seen nothing." Nearly everyone seems to find this fishing town east of Marseille to their liking. Fishmongers sell the fresh catch at market, alongside vendors with produce, cheese, breads, and souvenirs. Restaurants serve *bouillabaisse* and *moules frites,* and local vineyards produce well-regarded white and rosé wines that nicely complement the seafood. Rugged limestone cliffs from Cassis to Marseille are dotted with sheltered inlets (*calanques*). A scenic route twists up to the top of Cap Canaille and then heads east toward La Ciotat. If you take it, you're likely to feel on top of the world—and perhaps inspired to quote Mistral.

Truffle Markets

*Y*EARS AGO, when visiting Italy, I packed truffle oil to bring back for a friend. The bottle spilled, saturating my luggage with a musky aroma. Trust me, the scent loses its appeal when oil drips from your socks. I washed it out of my clothing, but the suitcase was a lost cause—as was my appetite for truffles. That is, until I visited the markets in Provence and devoured a truffle omelet in Richerenches.

Peasants dug up truffles as everyday food during the Middle Ages. That changed when François I liked them so much that he issued a *lettre de noblesse* declaring truffles a luxury product. Provence is the capital of the *Tuber melanosporum,* or black truffle. The *département* of Vaucluse produces 70 percent of the truffles in France, more than Périgord. "Périgord," when applied to truffles, is a botanical name and not a geographical description.

The quantity of French truffles has dropped from about 1,500 tons in the 1800s to roughly 30 tons annually now. Wholesale prices for the "black diamonds" fluctuate between 400 and 1,000 euros per kilo, depending on the season. Retail prices are double or triple.

Black truffle season runs from mid-November through March. It peaks in January and February. A local chef says that truffles dug up early in the season are less tasty. He won't even consider cooking with them until January. The best way to find black diamonds is to go on a hunt with an experienced guide (human, porcine, or canine) or head to the truffle markets. From mid-November through March, Richerenches has wholesale and retail truffle markets on Saturday from 9 a.m. to 1 p.m.; the Carpentras truffle market is Friday at 9 a.m. at the Hôtel-Dieu; Valréas has a Wednesday market, but only for wholesalers. It's not unusual to see chefs at these markets.

Christmas and Santon Markets

FOR SEVERAL WEEKS prior to Christmas, *marchés de Noël* begin popping up, with twinkling lights and chalet-style stalls. These specialty markets are full of good cheer, and there's plenty for everyone to enjoy regardless of one's religious beliefs. Vendors sell handcrafts, decorations, gourmet specialties, mulled wine, and sweets. The regular Provençal markets are well stocked with delicacies such as game, *foie gras,* smoked salmon, and black truffles, to make the holiday meal special.

Santons are integral to the Christmas decorations. "Little saints" in the Provençal language, *santons* are meticulously hand-painted figurines. A craft unique to Provence, the tradition began in 1789 when churches were closed and nativity scenes were forbidden. To circumvent these strictures, the Marseillaise artist Jean-Louis Lagnel (1764–1822) began creating miniature figurines at afford-able prices so that local worshippers could make *crèches* within their homes. Nativity scenes remain the most common form of the craft, with clay figurines depicting Mary and the baby Jesus, wise kings, shepherds, barnyard animals, and angels. The range

of *santons* later expanded to represent traditional Provençal trades and activities: fishermen, dairy maids, peasant women harvesting lavender, vegetable sellers with baskets of produce on each hip, mustachioed *boules* players, the village idiot (said to bring good luck), and bread bakers.

Santon fairs occur throughout Provence around Christmas. The largest *marché aux santons* takes place in Marseille from late November through December. There are also *santon* markets in Aix-en-Provence, Arles, Aubagne, and Avignon. If you're not in Provence around Christmas but are interested in *santons,* you can find them at *santonniers'* workshops (several in Aix-en-Provence, for example) and occasionally at flea markets.

Chef Cyril Glémot

Before opening a restaurant in Cairanne in 2010, Cyril Glémot was the acclaimed chef at L'Oustelet in Gigondas. A tall man with silver-rimmed spectacles and spikes of brown hair, he conveys an intensity that's softened by a sense of humor. Glémot was born near Paris and started working in kitchens there. He moved to Toulouse in southwestern France, then to Avignon, then to Gigondas, and now has a restaurant that's literally in the middle of a vineyard. Summing up his career path, he says, "I followed the wine!"

Glémot's early training was focused on mastering traditional dishes such as *blanquette de veau*. "There is more room for creativity now. I'm glad to be part of a younger generation of chefs who play with flavors and textures. My brain is imprinted with dishes I've done before, but I'm constantly trying to innovate." One reason he enjoys his work is that it offers a chance to keep changing.

His menu shifts every few weeks to feature seasonal ingredients. He gets lamb from a farmer in the Alps, pork from the Drôme, and pigeons from a supplier in the mountains. Chef Glémot comes up with menu ideas by working with an energetic *sommelier,* Jean-Philippe Sebire. They taste wines and discuss which foods might pair well. "It's easier to start with the wine, pick out interesting notes, and then adjust dishes to complement those flavors," he explains. For example, a smoky wine with hints of anise inspired him to develop a dish of pork breast glazed with star of anise. The licorice flavors accentuate each other, and the pork's fattiness pairs well with a wine that has fullness in the mouth. "When I create a dish, it's very personal. I have to like it a lot." And so do many others.

Côteaux & Fourchettes is at Croisement de la Couran-çonne, 84290 Cairanne. Tel: 04.90.66.35.99. www.coteaux etfourchettes.com

Resources

Marjolaine
4,60 les 25g
Piment
3€ les
Sarriette
3€ les 50g
5,50€ les 100g

Local Food Specialties

Aïoli—Sauce made of garlic, olive oil, and egg yolks

Anchoïade—Spread made of crushed anchovies, garlic, herbs, and olive oil

Bagna cauda—"Hot bath" of garlic, olive oil, and anchovies as warm dip for bread or vegetables

Beignet—Vegetable or shellfish fritter

Bouillabaisse—A specialty of Marseille, fish stew made with bony Mediterranean fish in tomato and onion broth

Bourride—Fish stew similar to *bouillabaisse* but not so complicated or expensive

Brandade de morue—Creamy baked emulsion of salt cod, garlic, olive oil, and milk

Daube—Meat stew made with red wine, vegetables, garlic, and herbs

Escabeche—Poached or fried fish marinated in vinegar or citrus juice

Fougasse—Flat bread brushed with olive oil, often studded with olives

Chèvre—Cheese made from goat milk

Gardianne de taureau—Bull meat marinated in wine

Gibassier—Bread made with olive oil and orange zest

Herbes de Provence—Mixture of dried rosemary, thyme, savory, marjoram, and sometimes lavender

Pan bagnat—Crusty sandwich that's a specialty of Nice

Panisse—Crispy snack made from baked or fried chickpeas

Persillade—Minced parsley and garlic

Petits farcis—Eggplant, zucchini, or tomato stuffed with seasoned minced meat

Pissaladière—Pizzalike tart of onions, black olives, and anchovies

Pistou—Sauce made of basil, garlic, and olive oil

Ratatouille—Vegetable stew of tomato, eggplant, zucchini, pepper, onion, garlic, and olive oil

Rouille—Spicy saffron sauce typically added to fish soup such as *bouillabaisse*

Saucisson d'Arles—Pork and beef sausage seasoned with red wine, garlic, and peppercorns

Socca—Chickpea flour pancake that's a specialty of Nice

Tapenade—Crushed black or green olives mixed with capers, garlic, and olive oil

Tian—Layered casserole of vegetables topped with cheese

Trouchia—Chard and onion omelet

Restaurants

Some of the best are perched on hillsides or tucked amid vineyards. Many have only a handful of tables and are operated by a staff of two (generally a husband and wife): One stays in the kitchen while the other tends to customers. Menu choices are limited, but the food rarely disappoints. It's not necessary to spend a lot for a good meal. Prix-fixe menus offer the best value. Prices are often lower at lunch. Popular restaurants fill up fast, so call in advance to reserve whenever possible. It's an ever-changing scene with new restaurants opening and chefs moving around. Here are a few of the many possibilities at various price points. *Bonne chance* and *bon appétit!*

AIX-EN-PROVENCE
Le Poivre d'Ane (40 Place des Cardeurs). Tel: 04.42.21.32.66
Les Deux Garçons (53 Cours Mirabeau). Tel: 04.42.26.00.51

ANSOUIS
La Closerie (Boulevard des Platanes). Tel: 04.90.09.90.54

ARLES
L'Atelier de Jean-Luc Rabanel (7 Rue des Carmes).
  Tel: 04.90.91.07.69
L'Estrambord (7 Route Abrivado Sambuc). Tel: 04.90.97.20.10

AVIGNON

Christian Etienne (10 Rue de Mons). Tel: 04.90.86.16.50

L'Essential (2 Rue de la Petite Fusterie). Tel: 04.90.85.87.12

La Mirande (4 Place de l'Amirande). Tel: 04.90.14.20.20

Les 5 Sens (18 Rue Joseph Vernet). Tel: 04.90.85.26.51

BONNIEUX

Auberge de l'Aiguebrun (Domaine de la Tour).
    Tel: 04.90.04.47.00

L'Arôme (2 Rue Lucien Blanc). Tel: 04.90.75.88.62

La Bastide de Capelongue (Chemin des Cabanes).
    Tel: 04.90.75.89.78

Le Fournil (5 Place Carnot). Tel: 04.90.75.83.62

BUOUX

Auberge de la Loube (Quartier la Loube). Tel: 04.90.74.19.58

CADENET

Auberge La Fenière (Route de Lourmarin).
    Tel: 04.90.68.11.79

CAIRANNE

Côteaux & Fourchettes (Croisement de la Courançonne).
    Tel: 04.90.66.35.99

CASENEUVE

Le Sanglier Paresseux (HLM St. François). Tel: 04.90.75.17.70

CRESTET

    La Fleur Bleue (Chemin de Sublon). Tel: 04.90.36.23.45

CUCURON

    La Petite Maison de Cucuron (Place Étang).
        Tel: 04.90.68.21.99

EYGALIÈRES

    Sous les Micocouliers (Traverse Montfort).
        Tel: 04.90.95.94.53

FONTVIEILLE

    Le Bistrot Mogador (Château d'Estoublon on Route de
        Maussane). Tel: 04.90.54.64.00

GARGAS

    La Coquillade (Le Perrotet). Tel: 04.90.74.71.71

GORDES

    La Bastide de Gordes (Route de Come). Tel: 04.90.72.12.12
    Le Mas Tourteron (Chemin de Sainte Blaise les Imberts).
        Tel: 04.90.72.00.16

GOULT

    Café de la Poste (Rue de la République).
        Tel: 04.90.72.23.23
    La Bartavelle (Rue du Cheval Blanc). Tel: 04.90.72.33.72

LAGARDE-D'APT

Le Bistrot de Lagarde (RD 34). 04.90.74.57.23

L'ISLE-SUR-LA-SORGUE

Le Carré d'Herbes (13 Avenue des Quatre Otages).
Tel: 04.90.38.23.97
Le Jardin du Quai (91 Avenue Julien Guigne).
Tel: 04.90.20.14.98
Le Vivier (800 Cours Fernande Peyre). Tel: 04.90.38.52.80
Umami (33 Rue Carnot). Tel: 04.90.20.82.12

LOURMARIN

La Louche à Beurre (Route d'Apt). Tel: 04.90.68.00.33
Le Mas de Guilles (Route de Vaugines). Tel: 04.90.68.30.55
Le Moulin de Lourmarin (Rue du Temple).
Tel: 04.90.68.06.69

MAUBEC

La Maison Gouin (44 Route d'Apt). Tel: 04.90.76.90.18

MÉNERBES

Café Véranda (Avenue Marcellin Poncet). Tel: 04.90.72.33.33
Maison de la Truffe et du Vin du Luberon (1 Place Horloge).
Tel: 04.90.72.38.37

MÉRINDOL

La Bastide du Grand Tilleul (1 Avenue des Bruillères).
Tel: 04.32.50.20.82

MOLLÉGÈS
Mas du Capoun (27 Avenue des Paluds). Tel: 04.90.26.07.12

MONDRAGON
La Beaugravière (RN 7). Tel: 04.90.40.82.54

NYONS
Le Verre à Soie (12 Place Docteur Bourdongle).
Tel: 04.75.26.15.18

PARADOU
Le Bistro du Paradou (57 Avenue de la Vallée des Baux).
Tel: 04.90.54.32.70

PERNES-LES-FONTAINES
Au Fil du Temps (51 Place Louis Giraud). Tel: 04.90.30.09.48

RICHERENCHES
O'Rabasse (5 Place de la Pompe). Tel: 09.52.97.34.93

ROUSSILLON
Restaurant David (Place de la Poste). Tel: 04.90.05.60.13
Le Piquebaure (Les Estrayas). Tel: 04.32.52.94.48

SAIGNON
Le Comptoir de Balthazar (Place de l'Église).
Tel: 04.90.04.63.55

SAINT-MARTIN-DE-LA-BRASQUE
Restaurant de la Fontaine (Place de la Fontaine).
Tel: 04.90.77.02.66.

SAINT-RÉMY
Le Mas de l'Amarine (Ancienne Voie Aurélia).
Tel: 04.90.94.47.82
Maison Drouot (150 Route de Maillane).
Tel: 04.90.15.47.42

SORGUES
La Table de Sorgues (Rue du 19 Mars 1962).
Tel: 04.90.39.11.02

VAISON-LA-ROMAINE
Bistro du'O (Rue du Château). Tel: 04.90.41.72.90

VILLENEUVE-LÈZ-AVIGNON
Restaurant le 7 (1 Rue des Frères Reboul).
Tel: 06.84.80.17.27

x du jardin

au jardin (classe-promenad

les petits pois

le chou

les salades

la ro

rottes

les tomates

les navets

les radis

e des légumes (pommes de terre, haricots, petits pois, etc...) et

la poire

les cerises

la pêche

les abricots

les fraises

le raisin

les groseilles

les noix

des fruits mais il faut détruire les animaux nuisibles com

Useful Market Phrases

I'm just looking, thanks	*Je regarde, merci*
How much is that?	*C'est combien?*
Could you possibly give me a better price?	*Pourriez-vous me faire un meilleur prix?*
I'll think about it	*Je vais y penser*
I'd like that one	*Je voudrais ça, s'il vous plaît*
Are they very fresh?	*Sont-ils bien frais?*
About 2 pounds	*Un kilo*
About 1 pound	*Un demi-kilo*
Three slices	*Trois tranches*
A good handful	*Une bonne poignée, s'il vous plaît*
I'd like two of them	*J'en voudrais deux*
Half that much	*La moitié de ça, s'il vous plaît*
A bit more	*Encore un peu*
A bit less	*Un peu moins*

That's enough, thanks	*Ça suffit comme ça, merci*
Too big/small	*Trop grand/petit*
That's perfect	*C'est parfait*
Do you have a bag?	*Avez-vous un sac?*
Is there a café nearby?	*Y a-t'il un café tout près?*
I'm looking for a toilet	*Les toilettes, s'il vous plaît?*
What time do you close?	*A quelle heure ça ferme?*
Thanks for your help	*Merci bien; c'est gentil*
See you again next week	*À la semaine prochaine*

Index

Acknowledgments

Researching and writing about the markets of Provence has been immensely pleasurable to say the least, though also a Herculean effort. I couldn't have done it without the generous help of others.

Dixon Long encouraged me to write this book and contributed his expertise from start to finish. He helped me shape the structure, decide which markets to include, edit drafts, and answer questions that arose while I was in Provence and after I returned home for the writing. His *Markets of Provence* was a touchstone and inspiration, and his contributions to this one are so significant that he deserves special mention.

My agent, Joy Tutela, has guided this project with vision and passion. BJ Berti, my editor, and the team at St. Martin's Press embraced it with gusto and made it much better.

Mélody Raynaud and Valérie Gillet provided assistance that became the turning point in bringing the idea to fruition. My thanks to Marion Fourestier, Katherine Johnstone, Valérie Bisset, Marion Nicoletti, Francine Riou, Marie Chatelain, Maryline Faubet, Martine DiCicco, Marie Gendebien, Loïc Falcher, Martine Favras, Elsa Aptel, Amandine Thirot, Sylvie Chapon, Jérôme Pons, Yannick Frizet, Benjamin Houdan, Stéphanie Nagne, and Florence Nochez. Sharon deRham, an ace tour guide, has become an advisor and friend, Kelly McAuliffe and Michel Blanc introduced me to the local wines. Carolyn Faure was an effective ambassador for Provence even as she turned her sights toward Paris. Julie Battilana and Romain Aubanel inspired me with their memories of growing up around these markets. Mike and Julia Roberts road-tested itineraries and gathered material to fill a few holes. Marilyn and Jim Reynolds welcomed me to Mas de la Perdrix (which I recommend to anyone looking for a dreamy stay near Roussillon). Anthony Mehran Khoi generously arranged an unforgettable stay in Gordes. Christian and Paola Deferry provided meals and friendship that kept me well nourished.

I'm grateful to the farmers and chefs who carved time out of their schedules to talk with me, and also to the market vendors, shopkeepers, and others who helped deepen my understanding of Provence, including Hélène Michel, Jean-Marie Reissi, Sylvie Santos, Yann Jouët, Caroline Missoffe, Pierre Chabert, Sabine Vallette, Dominique Damiano, Thibaud Boyer, Elodie Piton, Jérôme Campanelli, Jonathan Chiri, Josiane Déal, Gilles Peyrerol, Elodie Burgé, Claudine Vigier, Lucette Guglielmino, Guillaume Liardet, Eric Sapet, Ugo van Hulsen, Aftab Badyari, André Charransol, and Jean-Marie Valayer. I hope this book returns the favor. The sellers whose names I never learned—the hat vendor, the potter, the lavender merchant who introduced me to Gilbert Bécaud songs—thanks for the friendly welcome as I appeared at one market after another. Now you know why.

I am blessed with many wonderful friends and family. Robin Heyden helped get this project off to a running start when she joined me on the initial research trip and continued contributing advice until it crossed the finish line. Plynn Guttman coached me on how to keep it manageable *and* fun. Mission accomplished! Beth Grossman is an angel who makes good things happen, always. Carol Franco's unerring publishing instincts and friendship are incredible supports. Marni Clippinger gave me a gift that transformed my life. Rachel Schwartz, Lucie Leblanc, and Errin Douglas lent their creative talents to helping select visuals, and Stewart Clemens jumped to my aid when I needed assistance in preparing the photographs for production. The Wild Women made sure I didn't take anything too seriously. My gratitude to Jason Gerdom, Jennifer Danker, Kharma Finley-Wallace, and Nina Mullaney for supporting me with their technical prowess.

Most of all, thanks to Michael for being the best research assistant, life partner, and Chief Embarrassment Officer. Though I usually dodge the question of which are my favorite markets, the truth is they're the ones we explore together.

About the Author

Marjorie R. Williams writes about food and travel. She is co-author and photographer of *Markets of Paris, 2nd edition* (The Little Bookroom, 2012). She explores food, antiques, and craft markets wherever she goes. Marjorie lives in Cambridge, Massachusetts. www.marjorierwilliams.com

Photo by Valérie Gillet

Her indispensable advisor on this book, *Dixon Long,* coauthored *Markets of Provence* (1996) and *Markets of Paris.* A novelist and travel writer, he lives in Mill Valley, California. www.dixonlong.com

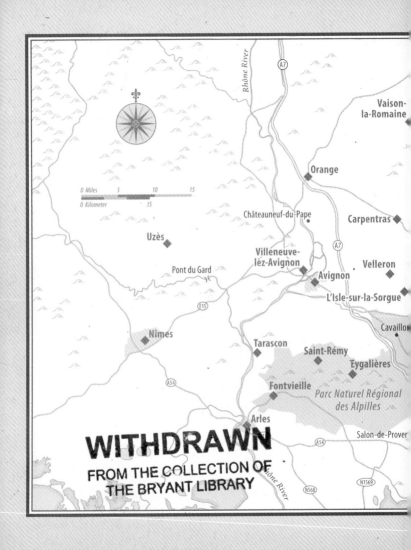